Environmental Decay in Its Historical Context

Edited by

Robert Detweiler
California State University, San Diego

Jon N. Sutherland
California State University, San Diego

Michael S. Werthman

Scott, Foresman and Company
Glenview, Illinois   London

The Scott, Foresman

TOPICS IN COMPARATIVE HISTORY SERIES
Michael S. Werthman, General Editor

Topics in the series:

BUREAUCRACY IN HISTORICAL PERSPECTIVE
Michael T. Dalby, Michael S. Werthman

COMPARATIVE CONCEPTS OF LAW AND ORDER
Jon N. Sutherland, Michael S. Werthman

ENVIRONMENTAL DECAY IN ITS HISTORICAL CONTEXT
Robert Detweiler, Jon N. Sutherland, Michael S. Werthman

Foreword

Topics in Comparative History is a series of anthologies intended to supply instructors and students with a new tool for the study of human institutions. The theme of the series is the diversity and comparability of significant elements in history.

The series represents a departure from the theoretical foundations of other, more traditional books of readings. It is not our intention to offer yet another collection of description and analysis of dynasties, commentary on the role of specific personalities, or recital of important events and dates. Rather, this series tries to sensitize students to the institutional dimensions of human history. Books devoted to problems, cases, or issues can be of use in the study of history, but it is not always possible to carry the lessons of such study over to other historical developments. Institutions are not abstractions. They are concrete and identifiable components of human society—past, present, and often future. Institutions may be defined and minutely characterized so that their presence and influence can be determined in the course of the students' researches. This institutional approach can be more productive of mature judgments than the study of such amorphous themes as the Renaissance. It is the aim of the series to help train students in understanding—not memorization—of the topic, in itself one of the highest goals of college instruction.

The series employs the comparative method, by which each topic is placed in historical perspective through descriptions of its nature and development in various times and places. When students see an institution functioning in different societies, they become more aware of the variations possible in comparable institutions. This wider perspective enables them to probe more intelligently their own history, society, and culture.

The volumes in this series will also allow instructors and students to incorporate their own special interests into various courses. Either whole volumes or individual chapters can be selected to accompany and supplement general textbook sections, thus facilitating more penetrating exploration by students into topics of particular interest and freeing instructors to be more interpretive in their lectures. Selections are by writers whose knowledge of the topic and whose aptness of style guarantee the students' surest acquisition of information that will be of the greatest significance and utility in their studies.

The most enduring value of the topics in comparative history series is its concentration on institutions and not merely on issues. Even the most glamorous and seemingly significant issues come and go, but by studying human institutions, students gain the ability to deal with any issue in any historical or social context. Issues, problems, and cases in historical development are relatively evanescent when compared with institutions, the persistence of which makes mastery of their nature and meaning one of the basic tools of historical scholarship.

Instructional materials should mirror the richness and scope of human history, and yet must also instill self-confidence in the students attempting to assimilate such a complex subject. The comparative study of institutions which this series offers can provide techniques for perceiving the variations in institutional history. Oversimplification, mere labeling, and memorization lose their attraction. The sophistication so acquired can be a permanent contribution to students' skills in research and analysis.

Michael S. Werthman
General Editor

Preface

The evidence of human enterprise is discernible throughout the world. Skyscrapers, high dams, supersonic aircraft, highway and railway networks are manifestations of humanity's persistent struggle to overcome time, space, and nature. The unmistakable signs of industry pervade every populated area, and flying over the countryside one notes how effectively people have turned much of the vast reaches of wilderness into neat, profitable units of food production.

This rather amazing achievement, the reshaping of the face of the Earth, rests largely on technology: the ability to devise and use tools. With tools people have performed the unprecedented feat of altering the character of their own environment. Many schools of historians have preached that humanity's record is one of progress, one of the key elements of this progress being a growing control over the Earth. Indeed, the notion persists that human beings can do anything through technology. This happy belief in our own unlimited creative potential has carried us through scientific, industrial, and technological revolutions; this faith inspired us to build our cities, reshape the landscape, and provide the abundance we equate with civilization and "the good life." And yet human creativity, when applied unrestrictedly, can also destroy the soil, fill rivers and lakes with wastes, and render the air all but unbreathable. In reshaping the Earth we wield the power to disrupt the natural order of things upon which human survival itself depends.

The grim fact is that our genius has created a grave crisis. For several hundred years we have been moving, slowly at first, and now rapidly, toward an ecological catastrophe. When the first clouds of smoke and soot bellowed from the industrial centers of Europe, "our effluent society" was born, to be cursed for generations by environmental violence and despoliation.

Human abuse of nature dates from prehistoric times, and the problem of environmental decay began with the advent of civilization. However, until a few generations ago the global environment had not yet been placed in jeopardy by the relatively small numbers of human beings possessing limited technological capacity.

Until rather recently, ecology meant very little to most of us. It was just another of the "ologies"—like paleontology, ichthyology, ornithology—the study of something very esoteric reserved for the ivory tower eggheads. All that is changed; ecology is now a term in common usage, a staple of popular journalism. Ecology stems from the Greek root *oikos*, meaning "house," and refers to the study of how living organisms and the environment function together as a whole. One might say it is the study of how people live in their "house" (their environment), how human beings interact with other organisms and the environment in the struggle for survival.

We have not been doing so well lately. Because of our profligate misuse of the environment, we too could become one of the endangered species. In Tokyo, a policeman must be relieved after only an hour of traffic control duty in the murky, smog-soaked atmosphere. The Rhine, "sewer of Europe," oozes its way through the industrial heartland of the Continent. Lake Erie is a cesspool containing so much sewage and industrial waste that life within it is all but impossible. The imperfectly purified drinking water of cities along the lower Mississippi has often been used over and over by industries and populations farther upstream. Within every industrialized nation ever-larger tracts of land are gobbled up to be covered with asphalt and concrete as the metropolis continues its inexorable expansion.

It is time to doubt our invincibility. The President of the United States made it clear that the challenge of this decade is the problem of environmental decay: "The great question of the seventies is: Shall we surrender to our surroundings or shall we make our peace with nature and begin to make reparations for the damage we have done to our air, to our land and to our water?" It is imperative to realize that *Homo sapiens* is but one creature in an interdependent community of living things. And this realization is required not only of idealistic students, but of the politicians, corporation executives, and consumers that students eventually become.

Environmental decay is not merely a topical problem, a "hot issue." It has an institutional dimension that justifies its inclusion in this series. The relationship between nature and humanity is both sufficiently ancient and structured to permit its treatment as an integral facet of human social behavior. And the consequences of our ignorance of this subject are more ominous than of our failure to understand less fundamental institutions.

The selections that follow provide an introduction to the historical record of human beings in relation to their environment and identify the historical roots of the present ecological crisis. Ours is the first generation to recognize, with increasingly knowledgeable concern, that we have taxed the Earth for centuries and that our assaults have been upon a finely balanced system that may not always be disposed to satisfy our nearly insatiable, usually brutal demands. Ours is the first generation to recognize, as U.N. Ambassador Adlai Stevenson put it, that "we travel together, passengers on a little space ship, dependent on vulnerable resources of air and soil; all committed for our safety to its security and peace; preserved from annihilation only by the care, and I would say, the love we give to our fragile craft." In that recognition there is misty hope for a quality life for humanity hereafter.

Human beings can become more genuinely creative by learning to be conservers instead of destroyers. In this spirit, the editors are pleased to state that this book is printed on 100% recycled paper and that a large portion of the royalties have been assigned to the conservationist Sierra Club. And because the environment is not the only victim of human brutality, the editors have avoided the use of sexist terminology in their introductions. However, the provisions of copyright law prevent our expunging sexist language from some of the anthologized selections. We consider this issue worth mentioning because the failure to resist the use of words that ignore or denegrate the female sex is a surrender to the same kind of institutionalized destructiveness that has so long encouraged the idea that earth, air, water, plants, animals, nature, even other people are for our use and misuse. As people learn to liberate themselves from such thinking, humanity moves closer to the ideals of rationality and compassion.

Robert Detweiler
Jon N. Sutherland
Michael S. Werthman

Contents

1
Human Attitudes Toward the Earth

Perhaps the most significant historical explanation of environmental decay is to be found in those attitudes that encourage people to exploit nature. Human beings alone have the power to change the Earth, and they are compulsive conquerors. They have proven to be one of the most destructive forces in all of nature. The relationship between human beings and the physical environment has been shaped by this human mania for domination—by a historically demonstrated compulsion to defeat and ravish the land, to subdue the Earth.

In the first selection that follows, John Storer examines the implications of this relationship and identifies a basic paradox. In the past one hundred centuries human beings have created civilized societies, and in doing so they have built in the capacity to destroy the life-giving environment that makes civilization possible. Ancient peoples used their intelligence to improve their lot; they mastered the use of tools, weapons, fire, and then they developed agriculture, which revolutionized life. Agriculture represented a new relationship with the environment that made it possible for people to live in increasingly large communities. The creation of city living was a crucial step in the separation of humans from nature. Civilized people living in large groups put far greater pressures on the surrounding land, vastly increasing the potential for environmental abuse through the undisciplined use of land and resources. Many once-fertile areas of the Earth have been so injured by civilized people that they have become virtual deserts, regions inhospitable to life where life had been so abundant. Storer shows that in Mesopotamia, one of the earliest centers of civilization, overgrazing of grasslands, overcutting of timber, overuse of agricultural resources contributed to the destruction of many of the first civilized societies. It is the terrible irony of human progress that civilized people have so overtaxed their environment that they have vitiated the life-supporting capacity of the land, the very thing that makes all civilization possible.

Fairfield Osborn looks at "our plundered planet" and gives some more recent examples that illustrate Storer's point that a dense population takes more from the land than the people put back. Osborn indicates that history sanctions the conquering of the Earth as humanity's right and destiny, as the reasonable outcome of the pitched battle with nature. Osborn agrees that population pressure has done irrevocable damage to the fertility of the land, as in Spain, where generations of migratory sheepherders overgrazed the land and upset the balance between humans and their environment. More recently, the impact of the sheep industry and land mismanagement in Australia has brought deforestation, destruction of the watershed, and a challenge to the life-support balance of that continent. Storer and Osborn agree that civilized people have taken for granted a human-centered existence.

Western peoples in particular have cultivated a dominance over their physical surroundings and a concept of the natural environment as being spiritually irrelevant. Lynn White, Jr. has traced the historical roots of the environmental crisis to the Judeo-Christian tradition, which he finds has encouraged an insensitivity toward nature and a god-like superiority over the nonhuman world. This Western moral attitude of dominion over the environment is firmly established in the creation story of the Old Testament. The lines of Genesis (1:28) allow for an attitude of human superiority and justification for exploitation of the environment: "Be fruitful, and multiply, and replenish the earth, and subdue it; and have dominion over the fish of the sea, and over the fowl of the air, and over every living thing that moveth upon the earth." White asserts that Judeo-Christian theology and Eastern religions present different views of human beings in relation to their environment and this difference is crucial in understanding the occidental sense of superiority over the land. In non-Western religious philosophy people see themselves as being a part of nature, that there is a continuity of self in all living things. Historically the Shinto belief, for example, is a simple nature worship by which the Japanese attribute diety to various environmental phenomena, especially the fertility of nature. Zen Buddhism appreciates the moral dimension of the relation between the human spirit and the natural environment. It is geared to a love for nature and a rustic simplicity with humans in harmony with their surroundings. On the other hand, the Judeo-Christian heritage denies the bonds of nature with the human spirit. The Western tradition teaches that human beings are the masters of nature and more akin to angels than beasts. White suggests that this heritage encourages an exploitative instinct and enhances an insensitive attitude toward abuse of the Earth.

In the final selection of this section, former Secretary of the Interior Stewart Udall traces the history of the relationship between the people and the land in America. He notes that the American Indians had a primitive reverence for the life-giving land and that they developed bonds of kinship with the environment. They had no concept that the land could be owned and exploited by the individual. But the European settlers brought their own concept of private land ownership and a determination to subdue the land. The newcomers quickly cultivated a spirit of wastefulness that was encouraged by the abundance of land and resources they found in this virtually unspoiled continent. Udall suggests that the "primitive" Indians understood the human-land relationship better than the "civilized" Europeans; they recognized that human beings are not outside nature.

John H. Storer

Civilizations and Deserts

Human life today is oppressed and distorted by the inherited mistakes of history. We can see a clearer picture of human nature if we watch it searching for civilization in its unspoiled primeval environment.

It was more than 17,000 centuries from the time when the ape-man made his first stone tools until the first evidence of dawning civilization appeared. Through that long interval man left few tangible records of progress. The changing size and shape of his head showed that his mental equipment was growing. The improving quality of his stone tools and weapons showed that he was putting this growing brain to work and that he was passing the results on to his offspring for the improvement of his culture.

In his caves, man was leaving the bones of animals he used for food. Changes in the types of these bones showed that he was developing skills as a hunter. The earliest bone collections showed that he was catching small, slow-moving animals. Later, the bones of larger, stronger animals showed that he was both improving his skills as a hunter and probably hunting in organized groups.

About 360,000 years ago, in a cave in Choukoutien, China, Peking man left the remains of fire, together with the broken and roasted bones of his fellow man. The use of fire must have given man a tremendous advantage in his struggle against cold and predatory animals and in his ability to prepare food and to use a wider variety of edible things. It lengthened his day through the hours when he could not be hunting outdoors, thus expanding his social life and his chances for planning and thought. The beautiful cave paintings of France and Spain tell us that, thousands of centuries later, he was already using his intelligence and imagination to create beauty and to convey ideas and knowledge.

Somewhere in this vast expanse of time he made one of his greatest forward steps when he used that imagination to organize sounds into meaning. With words he could not only visualize and clarify his own thinking, he could also exchange thoughts with his fellows and organize group action. Finally, between 10,000 and 9000 B.C., a few groups of the early men groped their way toward the great step that was to revolutionize human life. They discovered how to farm the earth, to make it produce more food, especially the cereals which could be stored for future use; they learned to domesticate animals that could turn the products of the earth into meat and bone, wool and leather.

From *Man in the Web of Life: Civilization, Science and Natural Law* by John H. Storer, pp. 33-44. Copyright © 1968 by John H. Storer. Reprinted by arrangement with The New American Library, Inc., New York, New York.

It has been estimated that an average human family, living by hunting and the gathering of wild foods, will require between ten and fifty square miles of land (depending on its productiveness), for their support. On the other hand, a farmer settled on rich, well-watered land like the Nile Valley can produce enough to support a thousand people per square mile. The knowledge of agriculture gave human life a new meaning. It was able to give man an entirely new relationship to his environment, including his fellow man—the most important part of that environment.

As a hunter requiring a large territory, man was necessarily limited to living in small groups, each defending its own territory and rejecting additions beyond a tolerable size. He had not yet evolved as a creature adapted for life in a large community. But with his ability to raise food in quantity, he was drawn by many forces into living in larger communities, and this raised some new problems.

The Near East, in those early days, offered resources that were especially favorable for the development of agriculture. Here there grew the ancestral forms of wheat and barley that could be bred into rich sources of food. Here also lived the wild ancestors of animals that would respond to domestication—the sheep, goat, pig, cattle, and wild ass—which were to be found in the uplands bordering the Syrian desert at altitudes of about 2,000 to 3,000 feet. At least three, possibly more, centers of human development began on the western slopes and valleys of the Zagros Mountains that border western Iran, in the hill country of Turkish Mesopotamia and on the South Anatolian Plateau. There is still much excavating and research to be done in this country. All of the ancient remains so far discovered indicate that, up to about 10,000 B.C., the people who lived here depended entirely on hunting and food-gathering for their subsistence.

Among the oldest ancient ruins is Jericho. It was occupied nearly continuously for several thousand years. In its different levels of occupation, the artifacts and other clues to human activities help to suggest some of the important steps in the development of its early culture. The site of what might have been a shrine shows a radiocarbon date of 9551 B.C.; the settlement grew up near an abundant spring. Stone tools and weapons indicate that, in the beginning, hunting and fishing still supplied a considerable part of the food. But sickle blades and querns, for grinding grain, indicate that plant foods were also being used. Clay-lined pits suggest the storage of foods as well. (It is interesting to note that, even with the availability of clay and fire, it was still to be thousands of years before the art of pottery-making was developed.)

At first Jericho was a small village with houses built of clay. During the 8th millennium B.C., it began to grow rapidly, which suggests that, by this time, agriculture, with the help of hunting and the gathering of wild foods, had become productive enough to support a growing population. Through the centuries the houses went through many phases of building and then rebuilding over the ruins of the old—the types of building changing as the years passed. At this time there was still no pottery, and during this prepottery era at Jericho there were twenty-two separate phases of building that could be distinguished in the excavations.

During the first three building phases, the town had no fortifications. Evidently, unhappy experience showed the need for protection, and tremendous efforts were later put into the building of fortifications. About 7100 B.C., the settlement was destroyed by fire. Following this there were four more rebuildings, and then the site was apparently deserted for a time. It has been estimated from the size of the ruins that the population of Jericho must at one time have reached about 2,000. The huge amount of labor that went into the erection and maintenance of the fortifications implies not only that there was an ample available labor force, but that there must have been an effective leadership to organize and direct it. To feed such a community there must have been a productive system of agriculture, and it is thought likely that there must have been some outside source of revenue, such as trade. The presence of nephrite and other green stones, together with sulphur, bitumen, salt, shells, and turquoise matrix suggests such sources of origin as the Dead Sea, the Red Sea, Sinai, and Anatolia.

Early in the 7th millennium B.C. a new culture was brought to the deserted site of Jericho. This occupation must have lasted for a long time. In some places there were as many as twenty-six layers of plaster floors superimposed one above the other. There were indications of concern with the supernatural.

There were shrines and many small figurines of animals and of the mother goddess associated with a fertility cult. There were a number of human skulls that may have been associated with an ancestor cult. The faces were modeled in plaster, with cowrie shells for eyes. Some were painted to represent hair, and in one case a face was supplied with a mustache. This prepottery period lasted well into the 6th millennium B.C. It was succeeded by a totally different culture that used pottery for the first time.

As new settlements arose with their local differences the remnants left by the human occupants helped to show the steps in cultural development. The spread of the different types of pottery helped to indicate the trade routes and outlined the interchange of cultural contacts. About the middle of the 5th millennium B.C. cast copper tools and weapons appeared, followed a little later by gold. It would be, however, some centuries before the advent of the age of bronze.

By 4000 B.C. villages were growing to the status of city-states, and with this growth came the need for better means of organization and government. This need may have been the inspiration for a system of writing. By about 3500 B.C. written documents began to appear in Mesopotamia. Based at first on pictographs, the script developed by the Sumerians evolved into systematic writing, and, with this, the enrichment of knowledge and thought and the enrichment of human culture took another great forward step. Knowledge and ideas could now be accumulated and communicated. Organization and control of great masses of people thus became possible. . . .

About 2400 B.C. a canal system was built that connected the Tigris and Euphrates rivers. This greatly increased the area of irrigated farming as well as the opportunities for trade and conquest.

The increasing contacts between the cities brought new problems into focus.

Religion, represented by both an ever-present god and a semidivine king, was a powerful stabilizing force within the city. But in relations with the gods of other cities the city god was less helpful. As Professor Mumford has pointed out: "In the early days at least in Mesopotamia and Egypt the gods were all mad—mad with the lust of power, the desire to control." "On the favored terms desired by gods and kings, no city could secure its own expansion except by ruining and destroying other cities." "Who was the enemy? Anyone who worshipped another god, who rivaled the king's powers or resisted the king's will."

In 2331 B.C. a powerful king, Sargon, set out to build an empire, conquering a huge area from the Persian Gulf to the Taurus Mountains and the Mediterranean. Throughout a reign of almost fifty years, he was engaged in almost continuous warfare, dealing with revolts, and attempting to establish peace and unity in the empire. He founded his own city of Akkad and attempted to rule by force, spreading garrisons over the land, tearing down the protecting walls of competing cities, and taking hostages. But the use of force only led to more revolts, and he later tried to build the personal loyalty of his subjects. He kept Nippur as the religious center and established a civil service of Akkadian citizens who served under a personal oath of loyalty to himself. The men who controlled the provinces and other important positions were all appointed from this group. Thus, toward the end of his reign, he succeeded in establishing a period of great prosperity with widespread trade and commerce.

But human relationships were still largely a matter of force and the exercise of personal leadership. For the next four hundred years the development of the region fluctuated between times of success and decay. Two great kings, Shulgi and Naramsin, were deified for their successful reigns, which included the building of canals and temples and the maintenance of order; even during these times of prosperity the region was under constant pressure from tribes of nomads who grazed their flocks in the uplands to the east and north. Seeking new grazing lands for their sheep and goats, waves of invaders spread into the country, fighting for control of the land, cutting off cities from their sources of food and from their trade routes. Thus, between the times of prosperity, there were periods of economic collapse and famine. Canals became filled with silt, farms deteriorated, and cities were destroyed or abandoned. Within a period of three years four different kings sat on the throne of Sargon's city of Akkad. Finally, in 2151 B.C., it was attacked by invading Gutians and destroyed so thoroughly that its site has never been discovered.

In 1894 B.C. a new force was born in Mesopotamia. A small religious center, which later came to be known as Babylon, lay between the Tigris and Euphrates. It had a favorable position for trade and agriculture, and the rivers made good defensive barriers on each side. A wall was built around the city together with a number of outlying fortresses. Through years of campaigning and the conquest and destruction of competing cities, the power of Babylon grew. During this turbulent century there was one period of twenty-four years when the neighboring holy city of Nippur "changed hands" no less than eighteen times.

In 1793 B.C. Hammurabi inherited the throne of Babylon. Destined to become one of the great monarchs of antiquity, he devoted the early years of his reign to building the strength of the city, carrying out internal reforms, rebuilding the canals that supplied water for neighboring cities and allying himself with some to conquer others. When the usefulness of an ally was ended, he might turn on it and defeat it (as in the case of Larsa) or destroy it when it failed to abide by the terms of a treaty.

In attempting to unify his empire, he found that an important problem lay in the diversity of religious beliefs. The Semitic sun-worship, for example, was alien to the nature religion of the Sumerians. Hammurabi found an ingenious way to solve this dilemma. At this time the language of the Sumerians was dying out in Mesopotamia, and, to preserve the old Sumerian legends, they were being translated into the Akkadian language, which was chiefly used for literature and diplomacy. He saw to it that, in the translation, Marduk, the god of Babylon, was given a special status. In this new version it was related that, in return for important service, he had been elected king of all the gods. In this way he received divine authority for his preeminent position and became an important influence in unifying the Babylonian civilization.

One of Hammurabi's great achievements was the establishment of a code of law for the government of his empire. There had been earlier local law codes as far back as the 24th century B.C. based largely on tradition or custom, designed to serve peace and justice and the satisfaction of the city god. Hammurabi's code had far wider application, applying to an empire. Its basic purpose was stated in the introduction: "When Marduk commanded me to give justice to the people of the land, and to let them have good governance, I set forth truth and justice to the people of the land and prospered the people."

One of the chief responsibilities of the state was the maintenance of canals and farmlands which were the foundation of the common welfare. The farmer, who generally worked the land under a yearly contract with its owner, was subject to a detailed system of penalties for failure to maintain the land in good condition or to handle it properly. Every holder of land was responsible for maintaining the bank of any canal that flowed past his fields. Especially heavy penalties were assessed if his failure to do so caused loss to other users of the canal.

After the death of Hammurabi in 1749 B.C., a series of invasions and revolts divided the empire, slowly cutting the trade routes which brought in timber, metals, and other important supplies. In the 16th century B.C. the Hittites, from beyond the Taurus Mountains, speaking an Indo-European language, attacked and plundered Babylon. Other invaders during the same century brought in the deadly horse-drawn chariot, a new weapon which was almost irresistible on the battlefield.

With constant warfare, farmlands and canals were neglected, food production dwindled, and several of the ancient cities were deserted. Toward the end of the fifteenth century B.C., Egypt, seeking to extend its power into Mesopotamia, and in search of allies, supplied gold to help with the restoration of Babylon and nearby cities, including Nippur, but as the years went by this supply dried up. The next

1,300 years saw a continuing struggle between Babylon, Egypt, Assyria, and other powers for mastery in Mesopotamia. During these years Babylon was captured no less than twelve times and more than once reduced to ruins. There were times of famine or siege when people were reduced to eating human flesh.

Finally, in 689 B.C., the Assyrian king Sennacherib stormed Babylon and attempted to wipe it out. Buildings and defenses were pulled down and burned, and the bank of the Euphrates River was altered to divert water onto the land, turning the whole area into a swamp. The city had ceased to exist, but the countryside still needed administration. The loss of the city had done nothing to lessen the opposition of the Babylonian people. Reconciliation seemed the best policy. Sennacherib's son married a Babylonian wife and adopted the worship of Marduk and other Babylonian gods, and in 680 B.C. he set out to rebuild the city on a grander scale than before. Within thirty years another Assyrian king returned to besiege the city. By the time it was captured the streets were piled with corpses and the starving survivors were eating human flesh. The Babylonian king set his palace on fire and died in the flames.

Now the tables slowly turned. The Medes, who had been building their numbers in Mesopotamia, joined with Babylon and began advancing into Assyrian territory. In 614 B.C. the Medes destroyed the Assyrian city of Assur together with its inhabitants. Two years later the Medes combined with Babylon to besiege and burn the Assyrian capital of Nineveh. In 607 B.C. the Egyptian Pharaoh Necho gathered his full army to protect his interests in Syria, but in 605 the Babylonian crown prince, Nebuchadnezzar, surprised him at Carchemish and annihilated the Egyptian Army. In 539 B.C. the Persian King, Cyrus of Anshan, with bribery and subversion, persuaded many of the local priests and princes to join him in overcoming the tyranny of Babylon. When he entered the city he was welcomed as a liberator. However, the Persian rule was oppressive and corrupt, and the land was ready to welcome Alexander the Great when he defeated the Persian Army and entered Babylon in 331 B.C.

Alexander continued his victorious way eastward to India and Bactria. He dreamt of plans for a sea route to Egypt and India. Returning to Babylon he started on a project for an enormous harbor and several dockyards for the building of a fleet. Babylon faced the prospect of again becoming one of the great cities of the world until, in 323 B.C., Alexander died of a fever.

The death of Alexander was followed by years of nearly continuous fighting for power among rival claimants until, by 309 B.C., Seleucus, one of Alexander's officers, had gained control. He faced the Herculean task of rebuilding the city from an enormous mass of rubble left by the fighting. He also shared Alexander's vision of a sea route to India. For this purpose the Tigris would be a better river than the Euphrates. He decided to build a new city, Seleuceia, on the Tigris, about forty miles north of Babylon, and he went on to extend his empire as far as India. Babylon had sunk to a depopulated ruin.

[Babylon] was a city with fortifications that appeared impregnable. Within the walls were the temples of Marduk, Ninmah, Ishtar, and other gods, the great tower of Babel, 300 feet square at its base and nearly 300 feet high, the royal palace, with its fortified citadel, and the Hanging Gardens, celebrated as one of the seven wonders of the ancient world. Within the sacred precinct of Marduk was his shrine room, 130 feet long by 66 feet wide, the walls and roof beams plated with gold and precious stones. Herodotus mentions the gold altar, throne, and statues of the god, with a total weight, he was told, of more than eighteen tons. Beside this shrine were the chapels of other deities.

This tremendous work of construction tells of progress in the arts, science, and mathematics, the last of which used a system of roots and powers and decimals, a system superior to any other in the ancient world.

Through these centuries of change and development there were many changes in the world around Babylon. The forests were being cut on the upland hillsides for the making of buildings, for the baking of bricks, for the building of boats, and for shipment to Egypt which lacked timber. In the high country away from the fertile land of the great river valleys, tribes of nomadic herdsmen lived by raising sheep and goats. As they increased in numbers, beyond the carrying capacity of their grazing lands, they had to either destroy their grasslands through overgrazing or spread outward to find new pasture. This they did on a huge scale, moving back and forth over the face of southern Asia, often bringing their flocks to land already overgrazed by other occupants.

Sheep and goats can destroy the protecting grass cover on a hillside as effectively as a swarm of locusts. A look at the ruined lands in the American Southwest—the silted rivers and reservoirs—can give a graphic picture of the causes that lay behind the silting of the irrigation canals of Mesopotamia and of the pressures that drove the tides of nomadic invaders into Mesopotamia. Modern methods can partly repair the damage caused by misuse of land and, through wise use, can avoid further damage. But this requires organized discipline and motivation among the users of the land. This was lacking in the turbulent environment of Mesopotamia. The dawning of civilization had changed a small population that could live successfully off the land, into a greater population that was forced to overuse it and destroy its carrying capacity, fighting savagely in the process for ownership of what was left.

In the space of a hundred centuries man had come out from his early caves, learned how to make the earth productive, left step by step records of his rise in the understanding and mastery of his environment and in the creation of beauty and splendor. He had built the first civilization of history and then, through his multiplication and his instinct for aggression and personal dominance, he had pulled this great edifice apart, piece by piece, while at the same time he destroyed the foundation of natural resources on which the whole structure was built.

Out of this welter of obsolete instincts a few great leaders had arisen to build empires of disciplined peace and prosperity, empires that lasted only so long as the personal fire of the leader survived. Other civilizations, starting shortly after, were going through rather similar cycles of growth, experience, and decay—in Egypt, India, and China. Other leaders were promoting ideas which, as they spread, could discipline the human emotions more lastingly and effectively than those of generals and princes. Moses, in the 13th century B.C., brought down from the mountain the Ten Commandments given him by a single, all-powerful God. In India in the 6th century B.C., Prince Siddhartha Gautama, later known as the Buddha, preached a way of life that included in essence the spirit of the Ten Commandments. These two, followed a little later by Christ and Mohammed, spread ideas which have had more effect on human history than the greatest kings and generals.

Throughout the early attempts at civilization we see man searching for a solution to the paradox of human nature. Gifted with intelligence and reason, he finds these powers nullified by an instinctive driving force that is stronger than reason. To this day the search continues for some effective basis for a civilizing motivation that can be built into human culture and carried forward from generation to generation. Here lies the key to the search for civilization.

Fairfield Osborn

Our Plundered Planet

European peoples became intelligent tillers of the soil, and were not nomadic but lived for generations in one place. They loved their land and learned to return to it much of the substance they drew from it. It early became axiomatic to use manure to the fullest possible extent, and today in France and northern Italy you may see farmers sprinkling their hayfields with liquid manure before a rainstorm, and collecting from the public roads every scrap of animal refuse to add to the compost heaps that are a feature of nearly every household. With this sort of intelligent care the soil of a region may be kept in a condition of health and productivity indefinitely, as has been done in many parts of Europe.

Not all of Europe, however, has been so fortunate. In some places, particularly on coastal plains lying below mountain ranges, cultivation of the soil has been practiced on unterraced slopes that have gradually become eroded during the seasons of heavy rainfall. An outstanding illustration of this, within historic times, is provided in Italy by the Pontine Marshes. Originally this was a region of fertile farms. These marshes resulted from putting the surrounding mountain slopes to cultivation in an effort to feed the growing population in the days when Rome was a great power. Gradually those who lived on the coastal plains had to move away from their formerly productive lands, for their streams became choked with silt that washed down from the country above them, and in time a large part of the coastal area became a malarial swamp which threatened the health of all those who lived nearby. One of the causes of the fall of Roman civilization may well have been the declining health of Rome's people, resulting in turn, and to some degree, from the misuse of her land..The Pontine Marshes covered a large area where as many as sixteen towns had prospered before the rise of Rome to power.

For centuries after their formation the marshes remained a virulent breeding ground of pestilence. From the fourth century A.D. until the twentieth century the marshland defied every attempt made by man to reclaim it. Emperors and Popes in long succession tried what skills they had against the dangerous wasteland, but with no results of any lasting significance. Finally in 1931, owing to modern engineering skill, scientific knowledge, the expenditure of huge funds and a number of years of heavy labor, the marshes were at last cleared and reconverted into fertile and healthy land. They illustrate only too well the vast effort required to restore what man has ruined.

The incident of the Pontine Marshes illustrates another thing, the insidious danger to any part of the world where too many try to live on a land of limited production—for all land, however fertile and well cared for, is bound to be limited in its production. In a country like Italy, where the population pressure is about 830 people per square mile of cultivated land, the country is almost certain to suffer. People not only take more from the soil than they can put back, but they set about clearing more land on slopes above the plains, and thus release the force of heavy rains which in a few seasons, or even a single season, not only can destroy the new-cleared areas but can bury or ruin with debris all the fertile tracts below on the plains. Where plains lie at the foot of steep mountains, and where populations are too great, this is almost certain to happen. It has happened in many parts of Europe, in France as well as in Italy, and too often men have tried to curb the inevitable result by setting up a sort of warfare against nature. They build runoff channels and dams and spillways to carry away the excess water of the rainy months, and to protect the lower lands from erosion or from being covered with erosive material. They do what they can, often very effectively, to prevent the loss of life which so often accompanies floods and torrential runoffs. But this system of pitched battle with nature is in effect a treatment of symptoms rather than causes. It is like attempting to cure a person who is very ill, instead of attempting to prevent the illness in the first place. Treatment of symptoms is suggestive of a form of conflict. The handling of first causes, on the other hand, may be considered as a sort of friendly relationship, the forestalling of difficulties before they occur, the getting along with nature, instead of fighting with her after she is in revolt. Man must somehow, before it is too late, realize that he is part of nature, and that nature is not his enemy, for it is only by adjustment to the processes of nature that man, like all other living creatures, can establish a friendly balance that will make life on this planet possible for generations not yet born.

It is not invariably true, however, that population pressures result in damage to the fertility of the land. Even within Italy today there are regions, notably portions of the Lombardy plains, where the health of the land has been guarded for centuries. In Japan, no larger than the state of Montana but with a population one half that of the United States, the people with meticulous care, skill and intelligence have maintained the relatively limited amount of arable land that country possesses, only one fifth of its total land area, in a condition of productivity. But these instances, together with but a few others, are the exception to the general rule. They are encouraging as proof of what can be done.

Mahomet is supposed to have believed that the plow brought servitude and shame to mankind, and perhaps this Eastern idea, and the nomadic life it implied, had something to do with the almost unbelievable waste of fertile land in Spain. The great Spanish painters of earlier days depicted stark and fantastically beautiful Spanish cities built on rocky crags above wasted and gullied slopes. No one sensitive to the welfare of the land can look at these pictures without a feeling of foreboding. The plight of Spain today is exactly what one might suppose it would be, considering the plight of the land itself. The desperate and degraded condition of the countryside came about more through greed than through need, and its history dates back to the days when Spain was powerful and prosperous.

Before the fifteenth century there had grown up in Spain a vigorous and influential organization of migratory sheepherders, known as the Mesta. They moved their flocks northward in summer and southward in winter, over a land sparsely populated and at certain times threatened by Moorish invasions that tended to prevent settled populations from establishing themselves, especially in the lands towards the south. They had the land almost entirely to themselves, and followed stated routes for their migrations—long roadlike strips of grazing land where they were allowed to move freely as the seasons warranted. In their migrations they passed many communities which by law were permitted to fence in the "commons" or communal lands belonging to the villages, and these fenced places were, for many years, left undisturbed by the migrants. But the migrants had the privilege of cutting small trees and branches to supply their needs in fuel and fodder as they went along, and this seems to have been the beginning of misuse of the untenanted lands through which they passed. Orginally they were not considered hostile by the settled population, for their sheep in passing helped fertilize the fields, and after the grape harvest they not only enriched the vineyards but nibbled back the vines and thus saved many a vineyard owner the trouble of pruning.

When Ferdinand and Isabella came to the throne, however, they saw in the wool industry a great source of wealth for the crown and for their country, and they encouraged it beyond all other industries. Wool had high value in the foreign markets, and was compact and easy to ship, so in every way they could they encouraged the Mesta. Thus there sprang into being a number of laws and local regulations which favored the migrants against the settled population. The common lands in some cases were thrown open to the sheepmen, taxes for their use of their nonuse were levied, and the money collected reverted to the crown or to political become permanent owners of land belonging to others who had not happened to discover the presence of the squatters. Everywhere land was overgrazed, forests were burned off to provide extra pasturage, young trees were cut down for fodder or firewood, and the desperate cycle of greed and overuse and erosion was set into motion. The Mesta for a time exercised so great a power as a political organization that little or nothing could be done against it, and it continued long enough to ruin a large part of Spain. The same sort of migratory sheep raising had already produced havoc in South Italy and Tunisia, but the Spanish situation was more flagrant and more complete in its devastation of the land, which has not recovered since, and shows, after centuries, the plight of land misused by man. The final overthrow of the Mesta came about through political moves originated by the nonmigratory population, who were determined that they too should prosper by the wool trade, without the work and uncertainty of moving about from place to place. They stayed at home and raised sheep and levied taxes on the migrants, and carried on political and economic feuds which continued for many years. And so in the end the Mesta was overthrown, but not until it had in all too real a sense overthrown the balance of man and nature in Spain.

And there was a contributing factor: Spain became aggressive, and laid plans to become a great maritime power. To build her ships she cut her great trees, and the forests and all their related resources were sacrificed to the ambitions that promoted her trade. All this happened because of a combination of wish-for-power, greed, and lack of realization of the inevitable results that would follow the misuse of the land. In the light and knowledge of the present the whole senseless cycle of waste in Spain may look like something that adult human beings would never tolerate if they were aware of it. The terrible and pitiful fact is that the people of other countries are engaged in just this sort of wastage of their prime resources today. They—and this includes us of the United States—are too near to the picture to realize what is happening. . . .

Just as political influences, such as the Mesta in Spain, can result in great damage to the land, so can certain social customs. In the latter category one that deserves mention is the French system by which land, upon the death of the father, is usually divided up among the children rather than left to one child. This has resulted in land being cut up into smaller and smaller strips, until in some places a child's inheritance may be no more than a few yards in width or length. If the strips of land lie on a level, they may be in but small danger from erosion. But if, as often happens, they are on a slope, and the division of land results in strips running uphill, then there is great danger to the land, for heavy rains may cause rapid erosion. Strips of land must usually have access to a service road, and service roads are likely to lie along valley bottoms. Thus very often the land served by the roads is divided into uphill furrows, and unless the various owners agree to cut it up in a different manner and, by following the hill contours, to evolve a set of small terraces, no one can have much benefit from the land. The French Government some years ago set up a plan to build service roads so placed that horizontal rather than vertical division of the land could be achieved, and it also extended aid in financing the purchase of adjoining strips of land by individuals or groups, so that the land could be farmed in blocks rather than in strips. Where strips have been established that follow the contours of the land, the customary system of dividing land among the children has been a help to the land rather than a hindrance, and has resulted in much painstaking terracing and sluicing for surplus water runoff, and impounding of water for later use.

England has shared with western Europe a uniquely favorable record in maintaining her land in a fertile and productive condition despite centuries of use—in the main for the same reasons. Here, in addition, a social custom has played a helpful part, namely the passing of the ownership of land from one generation to the next by primogeniture, which has tended to prevent the division of land into small lots or strips as in France. Stone walls as well as thick hedges surrounding most fields have also contributed to the continuance of soil fertility, for there can be little erosion in closely walled fields. However, sheet erosion is not uncommon in England, while land deterioration from more active forms of erosion is quite general in the hilly country of Wales. In the face of such an apparently favorable situation it is the more startling to read the record of the debates that took place in the House of Lords during 1943 and 1944—held even during one of the most critical periods of the recent war. These debates reflected a growing apprehension that conditions were far from satisfactory as regards England's soil fertility in its relationship to the health of the English people. The speeches were punctuated by vigorous dispute as to whether "organic" or "chemical" methods provided the better solution to land restoration. A number of speakers voiced the opinion that there was something very wrong in the "life cycle" and that prompt action was needed "in order more definitely to establish the interrelation between morbid or deficiency conditions of soil, plants, animals and human beings." Reference was made to the increased decline of the water table and the extraordinarily low level of springs and wells. Attention was called to the fact that New Zealand and Australia had heretofore provided a very large proportion of the food on which England had subsisted in the past but that recent governmental reports from both those countries indicated that deteriorating land conditions had reached the point of being a grave problem, and that therefore England could not expect to receive imports of land products from either Australia or New Zealand equivalent to those it had received in the past. There was general recognition of the fact that the questions raised in the debate were extremely complicated in their nature and it was estimated that were a Report by the Royal Commission to be prepared, between ten and twenty years would be needed for its completion. Speakers for the government took a defensive attitude. They were not prepared to recognize the need for a special Report by the Royal Commission and the motion for its preparation was withdrawn.

In the meanwhile the processes of nature will continue to move upon their ordered courses.

The speaker who was troubled by the situation in Australia and New Zealand had good reason.

It has taken only about six generations to bring widespread conditions of land illness to Australia, as well as to New Zealand. This is fast work and almost equal in velocity and extent to the grievous injuries done to the land in the United States in a similar period of time. Australia and the United States are of almost identical size but all of the central part, amounting to about 40 percent, of the former country is a great natural desert. The United States is far more fortunate in that only about 14 percent of its area is desert and uninhabitable.

Some of the causes of land injury in Australia are identical with those found in other countries, such as the highly unfortunate destruction of forests which, to begin with, were very limited in extent, covering not more than 5 percent of the total area. Consequently Australia today is in the unnecessary and regrettable position of having to import more than 40 percent of its annual timber needs and considerably less than 2 percent of the country now has protective forest cover. Trees were regarded as an encumbrance by the early colonizers who were opening up the land for grazing and agriculture, and their devastating methods of burning the forests resulted in a vast amount of wasteful destruction. . . .

One of the most precious physical possessions of Australia is her rivers, dependent for their regular flow on the conservation of the forests in their watersheds. It is pathetic to look back and find that some of the early governors forbade the clearing of riverbanks and then to observe that these prohibitions were soon forgotten, so that in the second half of the nineteenth century tree destruction by burning or ring barking destroyed the forests on a gigantic scale. This deforestation has contributed to the loss of rhythm of the Murray, the greatest of the rivers of Australia, which is beset by alternating seasonal floods and abnormally low water.

For example, it has of late been observed that the low-lying lands on the coast of New South Wales, which originally were seldom subject to frosts, have, with the denudation of forests on the surrounding hills, experienced annual frosts, the probable explanation being that through the absence of trees the cold air of the highlands now flows unchecked and untempered down the sides of the hills to the valleys of the lowlands.

Then, too, Australia has suffered from the usual consequences of opening up lands to agriculture when proper land-use methods are not employed. For instance, the wheat lands of New South Wales are extensively and seriously damaged by erosion, owing partly to the fact that here wheat is often grown on undulating land with slopes of from 3 to 8 percent. Much of the land in New South Wales would now be recognized as too steep for cultivation and safer for use as pasture. In the hilly country of the coastal dairy districts, rapid erosion has followed the cultivation of corn and other fodder crops, and the situation with regard to water erosion in the cotton belt in Queensland is also a delicate one.

Serious wind erosion has occurred in the semiarid belt in the states of South Australia and Western Australia bordering the great central desert, partly because of the use of the land for growing wheat in regions in which there is extremely little rainfall. Here too there is the ever-present drifting of sand from the great desert.

There have been two other causes of serious land illness in Australia as well as

New Zealand. The first of these is the sheep industry, which, as is well known, has been developed to an inordinate degree. The other cause has every element of fantasy. This is the rabbit scourge, which is a stark example of the consequences that follow ignorance of the relationship of animal life with land health. The chain of events following upon the blind misstep of a handful of early colonizers, nostalgic for the pot-shooting amenities of their home country, verges on the incredible.

As to the sheep, there could be no situation that better exemplifies the dire consequences of overusing the land for purposes of trade or profit than that of the growth of the sheep industry in Australia, which has been an effort to gain from the land more than it is capable of producing. The origins of this industry from which, from a temporary point of view, the Australian people have gained such quick returns, but because of which the long-term or permanent health of the land has suffered so greatly, are worth a momentary review. In the early part of the nineteenth century England had become the world's most important center for the production of woolen goods and the spindles and looms of Yorkshire were demanding greater and greater quantities of wool. At that time English manufacturers were buying most of their wool in Europe either from the Spaniards or from the Germans. We have already seen the effect of the growth of the sheep industry in Spain under the Mesta and its effect upon that country. Spanish wool, however, was not retaining its quality and English buyers were switching to the wool of excellent quality that came from the Saxon Merino sheep. Woolgrowers of northern Europe, however, had to struggle with the rigors of a severe winter climate and this situation pointed the way to Australia's great opportunity whereby the then most wretched of British colonies could pay its way and even win its position as a commonwealth by contributing to the stupendous energy of England's economic expansion. By 1882, following a couple of decades of experimental breeding, the wool of Australian sheep was judged equal to the finest Saxon. The boast was made by Australian colonizers that their country "contained tracts of land adapted for pasture so boundless that no assignable limits may be set to the number of fine wool sheep which can be raised," and from that time on English manufacturers depended increasingly upon Australian wool and English capital assumed great influence in the development of this industry. In effect wool provided the economic-impulse that opened up the Australian continent and, incidentally, provided one of the reasons for the early overcutting of forests in the ill-considered attempt to get more pasture land at so great a cost to Australia's present-day land economy. Anyone who has not seen herds of sheep, each numbering several thousand animals, can form no conception of the damage to the land of which they are capable. Both sheep and goats are close-cropping animals and unchoosing in their readiness to eat all kinds of living plants, even to their roots. Further, plant cover that is not consumed is trampled and injured by the thousands of hoofs. When their numbers are not properly balanced or controlled, these animals are one of the major causes of injury to the surface of the land, of erosion and of eventual desolation. So it has been since before the days of Christ. So it has proved in many parts of Australia and of New Zealand.

It was a sorry day for Australia when an early colonizer from England packed a few innocent-looking rabbits aboard ship and sailed for his new home in the land "down under." This individual, whoever he was, together with occasional others who did likewise, has unwittingly cost the Australian people monetary losses that run into hundreds of millions of dollars and have caused injury to the land resources of Australia, much of it even of a permanent nature, that is beyond computation. Each and all of these men were blind to the fact that the predatory animals that existed in Australia, such as dingoes and several species of hawks, would be incapable of acting as automatic natural controls in keeping a rabbit population in balance. In passing, it should be noted that the subsequent importation of wild foxes, as a control measure, proved a complete failure. Nothing short of a thorough advance knowledge of the intricacies of wild life ecology could have prevented the avalanche of trouble that continues even to this day.

The first record of the existence of rabbits in a wild condition in any Australian state appeared in 1827, but the menace really dates from 1859 when the clipper *Lightning* arrived in Hobson's Bay with 24 wild rabbits for Thomas Austin of Barwon Park near Geelong. These were liberated and within three years rabbits first began to be referred to as a pest. Six years later Austin had killed off some 20,000 rabbits on his own and adjoining properties but was confounded at being forced to estimate that there were at least 10,000 left. At about the time of their introduction into Victoria there is recorded the ironical touch that a man was charged at the Colac police department with having shot a rabbit, property of one John Robertson of Glen Alvie, and was fined ten pounds, in accordance, no doubt, with the old poaching laws of England, where game was the property of the landowner. A few years later Robertson's attempt to stamp out the rabbits cost him £5000. Within the next thirty years the animals multiplied to such a degree and migrated so widely that they became a pest of the most critical kind practically throughout the entire Commonwealth. In the seven years from 1883 to 1890 the New South Wales Government was forced to spend not less than £1,543,000 in its attempt to control the scourge, and today rabbit control both in Australia and in New Zealand is a financial load upon every community. Many methods of eradicating this pest have been attempted. In Western Australia more than 2000 miles of fencing was erected at a cost of almost £500,000, but after it was all up it was found that some rabbits were already on the other side of the fence! Unfortunately, incidental to the compulsory use of poison for rabbits, there has been a very great destruction of wildlife as well as livestock, and phosphorus poisoning, employed for rabbit control, has been one of the principal causes of death among the marsupials and native birds.

The feeling of concern and apprehension regarding rabbits as a pest has even had psychopathic effects, as illustrated by the testimony of a witness before one of the parliamentary commissions who happened to live in one of the arid regions of South Australia where rabbits were a real curse. This witness stated that the rabbits in his part of the country had developed a long neck and miniature hump indicative of their capacity of living for long periods without water. These animals, when pressed to it, can live on bark and thus have been the cause of widespread killing of scrub growth by ring barking it, in addition to consuming millions of seedlings.

Another observer has pointed out that rabbits eat the hearts out of pastures by their habit of selective feeding, taking the best grasses and leaving the worst, and have in effect been the cause of creating new deserts. A writer in the Australian encyclopedia estimated that "with the removal of the rabbit the capacity of the Commonwealth in carrying livestock would be increased by 25 percent." This may be somewhat of an exaggeration, especially now that in the better pastoral lands the rabbit is fairly well under control. There are at least a few entries on the credit side of the rabbit ledger, such as the use of the animal for its fur as well as for its food value, as evidenced by the fact that in the decade ending in 1924, 157,000,000 frozen rabbits were exported and in the same period they exported more than 700,000,000 skins. But the harm done to both Australia and New Zealand by the unwitting actions of a few of the early colonizers is and will continue to be irreparable.

Lynn White, Jr.

On Christian Arrogance Toward Nature

A conversation with Aldous Huxley not infrequently put one at the receiving end of an unforgettable monologue. About a year before his lamented death he was discoursing on a favorite topic: Man's unnatural treatment of nature and its sad results. To illustrate his point he told how, during the previous summer, he had returned to a little valley in England where he had spent many happy months as a child. Once it had been composed of delightful grassy glades; now it was becoming overgrown with unsightly brush because the rabbits that formerly kept such growth under control had largely succumbed to a disease, myxomatosis, that was deliberately introduced by the local farmers to reduce the rabbits' destruction of crops. Being something of a Philistine, I could be silent no longer, even in the interests of great rhetoric. I interrupted to point out that the rabbit itself had been brought as a domestic animal to England in 1176, presumably to improve the protein diet of the peasantry.

From "The Historical Roots of Our Ecological Crisis," by Lynn White, Jr., *Science,* Vol. 155 (March 10, 1967), pp. 1203-1207. Copyright © 1967 by the American Association for the Advancement of Science. Reprinted by permission of the American Association for the Advancement of Science and the author.

All forms of life modify their contexts. The most spectacular and benign instance is doubtless the coral polyp. By serving its own ends, it has created a vast undersea world favorable to thousands of other kinds of animals and plants. Ever since man became a numerous species he has affected his environment notably. The hypothesis that his fire-drive method of hunting created the world's great grasslands and helped to exterminate the monster mammals of the Pleistocene from much of the globe is plausible, if not proved. For six millennia at least, the banks of the lower Nile have been a human artifact rather than the swampy African jungle which nature, apart from man, would have made it. The Aswan Dam, flooding 5000 square miles, is only the latest stage in a long process. In many regions terracing or irrigation, overgrazing, the cutting of forests by Romans to build ships to fight Carthaginians or by Crusaders to solve the logistics problems of their expeditions, have profoundly changed some ecologies. Observation that the French landscape falls into two basic types, the open fields of the north and the *bocage* of the south and west, inspired Marc Bloch to undertake his classic study of medieval agricultural methods. Quite unintentionally, changes in human ways often affect non-human nature. It has been noted, for example, that the advent of the automobile eliminated huge flocks of sparrows that once fed on the horse manure littering every street.

The history of ecologic change is still so rudimentary that we know little about what really happened, or what the results were. The extinction of the European aurochs as late as 1627 would seem to have been a simple case of over-enthusiastic hunting. On more intricate matters it often is impossible to find solid information. For a thousand years or more the Frisians and Hollanders have been pushing back the North Sea, and the process is culminating in our own time in the reclamation of the Zuider Zee. What, if any, species of animals, birds, fish, shore life, or plants have died out in the process? In their epic combat with Neptune have the Netherlanders overlooked ecological values in such a way that the quality of human life in the Netherlands has suffered? I cannot discover that the questions have ever been asked, much less answered.

People, then, have often been a dynamic element in their own environment, but in the present state of historical scholarship we usually do not know exactly when, where, or with what effects man-induced changes came. As we enter the last third of the twentieth century, however, concern for the problem of ecologic backlash is mounting feverishly. Natural science, conceived as the effort to understand the nature of things, had flourished in several eras and among several peoples. Similarly there had been an age-old accumulation of technological skills, sometimes growing rapidly, sometimes slowly. But it was not until about four generations ago that Western Europe and North America arranged a marriage between science and technology, a union of the theoretical and the empirical approaches to our natural environment. The emergence in widespread practice of the Baconian creed that scientific knowledge means technological power over nature can scarcely be dated before about 1850, save in the chemical industries, where it is anticipated in the eighteenth century. Its acceptance as a normal pattern of action may mark the greatest event in human history since the invention of agriculture, and perhaps in nonhuman terrestrial history as well.

Almost at once the new situation forced the crystalization of the novel concept of ecology; indeed, the word *ecology* first appeared in the English language in 1873. Today, less than a century later, the impact of our race upon the environment has so increased in force that it has charged in essence. When the first cannons were fired, in the early fourteenth century, they affected ecology by sending workers scrambling to the forests and mountains for more potash, sulfur, iron ore, and charcoal, with some resulting erosion and deforestation. Hydrogen bombs are of a different order: a war fought with them might alter the genetics of all life on this planet. By 1285 London had a smog problem arising from the burning of soft coal, but our present combustion of fossil fuels threatens to change the chemistry of the globe's atmosphere as a whole, with consequences which we are only beginning to guess. With the population explosion, the carcinoma of planless urbanism, the new geological deposits of sewage and garbage, surely no creature other than man has ever managed to foul its nest in such short order.

There are many calls to action, but specific proposals, however worthy as individual items, seem too partial, palliative, negative: ban the bomb, tear down the billboards, give the Hindus contraceptives and tell them to eat their sacred cows. The simplest solution to any suspect change is, of course, to stop it, or, better yet, to revert to a romanticized past: make those ugly gasoline stations look like Anne Hathaway's cottage or (in the Far West) like ghost-town saloons. The "wilderness-area" mentality invariably advocates deep-freezing an ecology, whether San Gimignano or the High Sierra, as it was before the first Kleenex was dropped. But neither atavism nor prettification will cope with the ecologic crisis of our time.

What shall we do? No one yet knows. Unless we think about fundamentals, our specific measures may produce new backlashes more serious than those they are designed to remedy.

As a beginning we should try to clarify our thinking by looking, in some historical depth, at the presuppositions that underlie modern technology and science. Science was traditionally aristocratic, speculative, intellectual in intent; technology was lower-class, empirical, action-oriented. The quite sudden fusion of these two, towards the middle of the nineteenth century, is surely related to the slightly prior and contemporary democratic revolutions which, by reducing social barriers, tended to assert a functional unity of brain and hand. Our ecologic crisis is the product of an emerging, entirely novel, democratic culture. The issue is whether a democratized world can survive its own implications. Presumably we cannot unless we rethink our axioms.

THE WESTERN TRADITIONS OF TECHNOLOGY AND SCIENCE

One thing is so certain that it seems stupid to verbalize it: both modern technology and modern science are distinctively *occidental.* Our technology has absorbed elements from all over the world, notably from China; yet everywhere today, whether in Japan or in Nigeria, successful technology is Western. Our science is the heir to all the sciences of the past, especially perhaps to the work of the great Islamic scientists of the Middle Ages, who so often outdid the ancient Greeks in skill and perspicacity: al-Rāzī in medicine, for example; or ibn-al-Haytham in optics; or Omar Khayyám in mathematics. Indeed, not a few works of such geniuses seem to have vanished in the original Arabic and to survive only in medieval Latin translations that helped to lay the foundations for later Western developments. Today, around the globe, all significant science is Western in style and method, whatever the pigmentation or language of the scientists.

A second pair of facts is less well recognized because they result from quite recent historical scholarship. The leadership of the West, both in technology and in science, is far older than the so-called scientific revolution of the seventeenth century or the so-called industrial revolution of the eighteenth century. These terms are in fact outmoded and obscure the true nature of what they try to describe—significant stages in two long and separate developments. By A.D. 1000 at the latest—and perhaps, feebly, as much as 200 years earlier—the West began to apply water power to industrial processes other than milling grain. This was followed in the late twelfth century by the harnessing of wind power. From simple beginnings, but with remarkable consistency of style, the West rapidly expanded its skills in the development of power machinery, laborsaving devices, and automation. Those who doubt should contemplate that most monumental achievement in the history of automation: the weight-driven mechanical clock, which appeared in two forms in the early fourteenth century. Not in craftsmanship but in basic technological capacity, the Latin West of the later Middle Ages far outstripped its elaborate, sophisticated, and esthetically magnificent sister cultures, Byzantium and Islam. In 1444 a great Greek ecclesiastic, Bessarion, who had gone to Italy, wrote a letter to a prince in Greece. He is amazed by the superiority of Western ships, arms, textiles, glass. But above all he is astonished by the spectacle of waterwheels sawing timbers and pumping the bellows of blast furnaces. Clearly, he had seen nothing of the sort in the Near East.

By the end of the fifteenth century the technological superiority of Europe was such that its small, mutually hostile nations could spill out over all the rest of the world, conquering, looting, and colonizing. The symbol of this technological superiority is the fact that Portugal, one of the weakest states of the Occident, was able to become, and to remain for a century, mistress of the East Indies. And we must remember that the technology of Vasco da Gama and Albuquerque was built by pure empiricism, drawing remarkably little support or inspiration from science.

In the present-day vernacular understanding, modern science is supposed to have begun in 1543, when both Copernicus and Vesalius published their great works. It is no derogation of their accomplishments, however, to point out that such structures as the *Fabrica* and the *De revolutionibus* do not appear overnight. The distinctive Western tradition of science, in fact, began in the late eleventh century with a massive movement of translation of Arabic and Greek scientific works into Latin. A few notable books—Theophrastus, for example—escaped the

West's avid new appetite for science, but within less than 200 years effectively the entire corpus of Greek and Muslim science was available in Latin, and was being eagerly read and criticized in the new European universities. Out of criticism arose new observation, speculation, and increasing distrust of ancient authorities. By the late thirteenth century Europe had seized global scientific leadership from the faltering hands of Islam. It would be as absurd to deny the profound originality of Newton, Galileo, or Copernicus as to deny that of the fourteenth century scholastic scientists like Buridan or Oresme on whose work they built. Before the eleventh century, science scarcely existed in the Latin West, even in Roman times. From the eleventh century onward, the scientific sector of occidental culture has increased in a steady crescendo.

Since both our technological and our scientific movements got their start, acquired their character, and achieved world dominance in the Middle Ages, it would seem that we cannot understand their nature or their present impact upon ecology without examining fundamental medieval assumptions and developments.

MEDIEVAL VIEW OF MAN AND NATURE

Until recently, agriculture has been the chief occupation even in "advanced" societies; hence, any change in methods of tillage has much importance. Early plows, drawn by two oxen, did not normally turn the sod but merely scratched it. Thus, cross-plowing was needed and fields tended to be squarish. In the fairly light soils and semi-arid climates of the Near East and Mediterranean, this worked well. But such a plow was inappropriate to the wet climate and often sticky soils of northern Europe. By the latter part of the seventh century after Christ, however, following obscure beginnings, certain northern peasants were using an entirely new kind of plow, equipped with a vertical knife to cut the line of the furrow, a horizontal share to slice under the sod, and a moldboard to turn it over. The friction of this plow with the soil was so great that it normally required not two but eight oxen. It attacked the land with such violence that cross-plowing was not needed, and fields tended to be shaped in long strips.

In the days of the scratch-plow, fields were distributed generally in units capable of supporting a single family. Subsistence farming was the presupposition. But no peasant owned eight oxen: to use the new and more efficient plow, peasants pooled their oxen to form large plow-teams, originally receiving (it would appear) plowed strips in proportion to their contribution. Thus, distribution of land was based no longer on the needs of a family but, rather, on the capacity of a power machine to till the earth. Man's relation to the soil was profoundly changed. Formerly man had been part of nature; now he was exploiter of nature. Nowhere else in the world did farmers develop any analogous agricultural implement. Is it coincidence that modern technology, with its ruthlessness toward nature, has so largely been produced by descendants of these peasants of northern Europe?

This same exploitive attitude appears slightly before A.D. 830 in Western illustrated calendars. In older calendars the months were shown as passive personifications. The new Frankish calendars, which set the style for the Middle Ages, are very different: they show men coercing the world around them—plowing, harvesting, chopping trees, butchering pigs. Man and nature are two things, and man is master.

These novelties seem to be in harmony with larger intellectual patterns. What people do about their ecology depends on what they think about themselves in relation to things around them. Human ecology is deeply conditioned by beliefs about our nature and destiny—that is, by religion. To Western eyes this is very evident in, say, India or Ceylon. It is equally true of ourselves and of our medieval ancestors.

The victory of Christianity over paganism was the greatest psychic revolution in the history of our culture. It has become fashionable today to say that, for better or worse, we live in "the post-Christian age." Certainly the forms of our thinking and language have largely ceased to be Christian, but to my eye the substance often remains amazingly akin to that of the past. Our daily habits of action, for example, are dominated by an implicit faith in perpetual progress which was unknown either to Greco-Roman antiquity or to the Orient. It is rooted in, and is indefensible apart from, Judeo-Christian teleology. The fact that Communists share it merely helps to show what can be demonstrated on many other grounds: that Marxism, like Islam, is a Judeo-Christian heresy. We continue today to live, as we have lived for about 1700 years, very largely in a context of Christian axioms.

What did Christianity tell people about their relations with the environment?

While many of the world's mythologies provide stories of creation, Greco-Roman mythology was singularly incoherent in this respect. Like Aristotle, the intellectuals of the ancient West denied that the visible world had had a beginning. Indeed, the idea of a beginning was impossible in the framework of their cyclical notion of time. In sharp contrast, Christianity inherited from Judaism not only a concept of time as nonrepetitive and linear but also a striking story of creation. By gradual stages a loving and all-powerful God had created light and darkness, the heavenly bodies, the earth and all its plants, animals, birds, and fishes. Finally, God had created Adam and, as an afterthought, Eve, to keep man from being lonely. Man named all the animals, thus establishing his dominance over them. God planned all of this explicitly for man's benefit and rule: no item in the physical creation had any purpose save to serve man's purposes. And, although man's body is made of clay, he is not simply part of nature: he is made in God's image.

Especially in its Western form, Christianity is the most anthropocentric religion the world has seen. As early as the second century both Tertullian and Saint Irenaeus of Lyons were insisting that when God shaped Adam he was foreshadowing the image of the Incarnate Christ, the Second Adam. Man shares, in great measure, God's transcendence of nature. Christianity, in absolute contrast to ancient paganism and Asia's religions (except, perhaps, Zoroastrianism), not only established a dualism of man and nature but also insisted that it is God's will that man exploit nature for his proper ends.

At the level of the common people this worked out in an interesting way. In antiquity every tree, every spring, every stream, every hill had its own *genius loci,* its guardian spirit. These spirits were accessible to men, but were very unlike men; centaurs, fauns, and mermaids show their ambivalence. Before one cut a tree, mined a mountain, or dammed a brook, it was important to placate the spirit in charge of that particular situation, and to keep it placated. By destroying pagan animism, Christianity made it possible to exploit nature in a mood of indifference to the feelings of natural objects.

It is often said that for animism the Church substituted the cult of saints. True; but the cult of saints is functionally quite different from animism. The saint is not *in* natural objects; he may have special shrines, but his citizenship is in heaven. Moreover, a saint is entirely a man; he can be approached in human terms. In addition to saints, Christianity of course also had angels and demons inherited from Judaism and perhaps, at one remove, from Zoroastrianism. But these were all as mobile as the saints themselves. The spirits *in* natural objects, which formerly had protected nature from man, evaporated. Man's effective monopoly on spirit in this world was confirmed, and the old inhibitions to the exploitation of nature crumbled. . . .

The Christian dogma of creation, which is found in the first clause of all the Creeds, has another meaning for our comprehension of today's ecologic crisis. By revelation, God had given man the Bible, the Book of Scripture. But since God had made nature, nature also must reveal the divine mentality. The religious study of nature for the better understanding of God was known as natural theology. In the early Church, and always in the Greek East, nature was conceived primarily as a symbolic system through which God speaks to men: the ant is a sermon to slug-gards; rising flames are the symbol of the soul's aspiration. This view of nature was essentially artistic rather than scientific. While Byzantium preserved and copied great numbers of ancient Greek scientific texts, science as we conceive it could scarcely flourish in such an ambience.

However, in the Latin West by the early thirteenth century natural theology was following a very different bent. It was ceasing to be the decoding of the physi-cal symbols of God's communication with man and was becoming the effort to understand God's mind by discovering how his creation operates. The rainbow was no longer simply a symbol of hope first sent to Noah after the Deluge: Robert Grosseteste, Friar Roger Bacon, and Theodoric of Freiberg produced startingly sophisticated work on the optics of the rainbow, but they did it as a venture in religious understanding. From the thirteenth century onward, up to and including Leibnitz and Newton, every major scientist, in effect, explained his motivations in religious terms. Indeed, if Galileo had not been so expert an amateur theologian he would have got into far less trouble: the professionals resented his intrusion. And Newton seems to have regarded himself more as a theologian than as a scientist. It was not until the late eighteenth century that the hypothesis of God became unnecessary to many scientists.

It is often hard for the historian to judge, when men explain why they are doing what they want to do, whether they are offering real reasons or merely culturally acceptable reasons. The consistency with which scientists during the long formative centuries of Western science said that the task and the reward of the scientist was "to think God's thoughts after him" leads one to believe that this was their real motivation. If so, then modern Western science was cast in a matrix of Christian theology. The dynamism of religious devotion, shaped by the Judeo-Christian dogma of creation, gave it impetus.

AN ALTERNATIVE CHRISTIAN VIEW

We would seem to be headed toward conclusions unpalatable to many Christians. Since both *science* and *technology* are blessed words in our contemporary vocabulary, some may be happy at the notions, first, that, viewed historically, modern science is an extrapolation of natural theology and, second, that modern technology is at least partly to be explained as an occidental, voluntarist realization of the Christian dogma of man's transcendence of, and rightful mastery over, nature. But, as we now recognize, somewhat over a century ago science and technology—hitherto quite separate activities—joined to give mankind powers which, to judge by many of the ecologic effects, are out of control. If so, Christianity bears a huge burden of guilt.

I personally doubt that disastrous ecologic backlash can be avoided simply by applying to our problems more science and more technology. Our science and technology have grown out of Christian attitudes toward man's relation to nature which are almost universally held not only by Christians and neo-Christians but also by those who fondly regard themselves as post-Christians. Despite Copernicus, all the cosmos rotates around our little globe. Despite Darwin, we are *not*, in our hearts, part of the natural process. We are superior to nature, contemptuous of it, willing to use it for our slightest whim. The newly elected governor of California, like myself a churchman, but less troubled than I, spoke for the Christian tradition when he said (as is alleged), "when you've seen one redwood tree, you've seen them all." To a Christian a tree can be no more than a physical fact. The whole concept of the sacred grove is alien to Christianity and to the ethos of the West. For nearly two millennia Christian missionaries have been chopping down sacred groves, which are idolatrous because they assume spirit in nature.

What we do about ecology depends on our ideas of the man-nature relationship. More science and more technology are not going to get us out of the present ecologic crisis until we find a new religion, or rethink our old one. The beatniks, who are the basic revolutionaries of our time, show a sound instinct in their affinity for Zen Buddhism, which conceives of the man-nature relationship as very nearly the mirror image of the Christian view. Zen, however, is as deeply conditioned by Asian history as Christianity is by the experience of the West, and I am dubious of its viability among us.

Possibly we should ponder the greatest radical in Christian history since

Christ: Saint Francis of Assisi. The prime miracle of Saint Francis is the fact that he did not end at the stake, as many of his left-wing followers did. He was so clearly heretical that a general of the Franciscan Order, Saint Bonaventura, a great and perceptive Christian, tried to suppress the early accounts of Franciscanism. The key to an understanding of Francis is his belief in the virtue of humility—not merely for the individual but for man as a species. Francis tried to depose man from his monarchy over creation and set up a democracy of all God's creatures. With him the ant is no longer simply a homily for the lazy, flames a sign of the thrust of the soul toward union with God; now they are Brother Ant and Sister Fire, praising the Creator in their own ways as Brother Man does in his.

Later commentators have said that Francis preached to the birds as a rebuke to men who would not listen. The records do not read so: he urged the little birds to praise God, and in spiritual ecstasy they flapped their wings and chirped rejoicing. Legends of saints, especially the Irish saints, had long told of their dealings with animals but always, I believe, to show their human dominance over creatures. With Francis it is different. The land around Gubbio in the Apennines was being ravaged by a fierce wolf. Saint Francis, says the legend, talked to the wolf and persuaded him of the error of his ways. The wolf repented, died in the odor of sanctity, and was buried in consecrated ground.

What Sir Steven Runciman calls "the Franciscan doctrine of the animal soul" was quickly stamped out. Quite possibly it was in part inspired, consciously or unconsciously, by the belief in reincarnation held by the Cathar heretics who at that time teemed in Italy and southern France, and who presumably had got it originally from India. It is significant that at just the same moment, about 1200, traces of metempsychosis are found also in western Judaism, in the Provençal *Cabbala.* But Francis held neither to transmigration of souls nor to pantheism. His view of nature and of man rested on a unique sort of pan-psychism of all things animate and inanimate, designed for the glorification of their transcendent Creator, who, in the ultimate gesture of cosmic humility, assumed flesh, lay helpless in a manger, and hung dying on a scaffold.

I am not suggesting that many contemporary Americans who are concerned about our ecologic crisis will be either able or willing to counsel with wolves or exhort birds. However, the present increasing disruption of the global environment is the product of a dynamic technology and science which were originating in the Western medieval world against which Saint Francis was rebelling in so original a way. Their growth cannot be understood historically apart from distinctive attitudes toward nature which are deeply grounded in Christian dogma. The fact that most people do not think of these attitudes as Christian is irrelevant. No new set of basic values has been accepted in our society to displace those of Christianity. Hence we shall continue to have a worsening ecologic crisis until we reject the Christian axiom that nature has no reason for existence save to serve man.

The greatest spiritual revolutionary in Western history, Saint Francis, proposed what he thought was an alternative Christian view of nature and man's relation to it: he tried to substitute the idea of the equality of all creatures, including man, for the idea of man's limitless rule of creation. He failed. Both our present science and our present technology are so tinctured with orthodox Christian arrogance toward nature that no solution for our ecologic crisis can be expected from them alone. Since the roots of our trouble are so largely religious, the remedy must also be essentially religious, whether we call it that or not. We must rethink and refeel our nature and destiny. The profoundly religious, but heretical, sense of the primitive Franciscans for the spiritual autonomy of all parts of nature may point a direction. I propose Francis as a patron saint for ecologists.

Stewart L. Udall

The Land Wisdom
of the Indians

In the dust where we have buried the silent races and their abominations
we have buried so much of the delicate magic of life.

—D. H. Lawrence (at Taos)

There are, today, a few wilderness reaches on the North American continent—in Alaska, in Canada, and in the high places of the Rocky Mountains—where the early-morning mantle of primeval America can be seen in its pristine glory, where one can gaze with wonder on the land as it was when the Indians first came. Geologically and geographically this continent was, and is, a masterpiece. With its ideal latitude and rich resources, the two-billion-acre expanse that became the United States was the promised land for active men.

The American continent was in a state of climax at the time of the first Indian intrusions ten millennia or more ago. Superlatives alone could describe the bewildering abundance of flora and fauna that enlivened its landscapes: the towering redwoods, the giant saguaro cacti, the teeming herds of buffalo, the beaver, and the grass were, of their kind, unsurpassed.

The most common trait of all primitive peoples is a reverence for the life-giving earth, and the native American shared this elemental ethic: the land was alive giving earth, and the native American shared this elemental ethic: the land was alive to his loving touch, and he, its son, was brother to all creatures. His feelings were made visible in medicine bundles and dance rhythms for rain, and all of his religious rites and land attitudes savored the inseparable world of nature and God, the Master of Life. During the long Indian tenure the land remained undefiled save for scars no deeper than the scratches of cornfield clearings or the farming canals of the Hohokams on the Arizona desert.

There was skill in gardening along with this respect for the earth, and when Sir Walter Raleigh's colonists came warily ashore on the Atlantic Coast, Indians brought them gifts of melons and grapes. In Massachusetts, too, Indians not only schooled the Pilgrims in the culture of maize and squashes, but taught them how to fertilize the hills with alewives from the tidal creeks. The Five Nations and the Algonquians of the Northeast; the Creeks, Choctaws, Chickasaws, Cherokees, and Seminoles of the South; the village-dwelling Mandans of the Missouri River country; the Pueblos of Hopi, Zuni, and the Rio Grande; and the Pima of the Southwest, all put the earth to use and made it bring forth fruit. Their implements were Stone Age, but most tribes were acquiring the rudiments of a higher civilization. They were learning how to secure a surplus from the earth, and were beginning to invest it in goods, tools, and buildings, and to devote their leisure hours to craft and art work and to the creation of religious rites and political systems.

The idea has long been implanted in our thinking that all American Indians belonged to nomadic bands that developed neither title to, nor ties with, the land. This is misconceived history, for even the tribes that were not village dwellers, tending garden plots of corn, beans, or cotton, had stretches of land they regarded as their own. But there was a subtle qualification. The land and the Indians were bound together by the ties of kinship and nature, rather than by an understanding of property ownership. "The land is our mother," said Iroquois tradition, said the Midwest Sauk and Foxes, said the Northwest Nez Perces of Chief Joseph. The corn, fruits, roots, fish, and game were to all tribes the gifts which the Earth Mother gave freely to her children. And with that conception the Indian's emotional attachment for his woods, valleys, and prairies was the very essence of life.

The depth of this feeling is reflected in the Navajos, who scorned the rich Oklahoma prairie country offered them by the government, and chose to live in their own arid and rugged deserts. It is reflected also in the Cherokees who, in the space of one generation, changed their whole way of life, established schools and libraries, produced an alphabet, planned a constitution and a legislature, and went to work in their own mills and blacksmith shops—all with the purpose of becoming so civilized that the whites would allow them to stay on their own lands and not ship them west to the Territories.

To the Indian, the homeland was the center of the universe. No member of a civilized people ever spoke of his native land with more pride than is apparent in the speech of the Crow Chief, Arapooish: "The Crow country," he said, "is exactly in the right place. It has snowy mountains and sunny plains; all kinds of climates and good things for every season. When the summer heat scorches the prairies, you can draw up under the mountains, where the air is sweet and cool, the grass fresh, and the bright streams come tumbling out of the snowbanks. There you can hunt the elk, the deer, and the antelope, when their skins are fit for dressing; there you will find plenty of white bears and mountain sheep.

"In the autumn, when your horses are fat and strong from the mountain pastures, you can go down into the plains and hunt the buffalo, or trap beaver in the streams. And when winter comes on, you can take shelter in the woody bottoms along the rivers; there you will find buffalo meat for yourselves, and cottonwood bark for your horses; or you may winter in the Wind River Valley where there is salt weed in abundance.

"The Crow country is exactly in the right place. Everything good is to be found there. There is no country like the Crow country."

Here is affection for the land, but no notion of private ownership. The idea that land could be bought and sold was an alien concept to the Indians of America. They clung possessively to certain chattels, but lands were nearly always held in common. An individual might have the use of a farm plot, but at his death it reverted back to the community.

The confrontation of Indians and whites had in it the seeds of hopeless misunderstanding from the start. The two cultures had produced irreconcilable concepts of landownership, and once the first white man set foot on American soil, the drama unfolded with all the certain sweep of a Greek tragedy.

Englishmen, especially, coveted land. It was something to be owned outright. Had not the English King given the charter deeds? The sixteenth-century Spaniard, by contrast, was not primarily interested in seizing land: the soldier wanted personal plunder; the priest came with his seeds and livestock to save Indian souls.

To the joint-stock companies of Virginia, intent on commercial profits, and to the colonizing Pilgrims, exclusive possession was the be-all and end-all of landownership. But the Indian's "title," based on the idea that he belonged to the land and was its son, was a charter to use—to use in common with his clan or fellow tribesmen, and not to *use up.* Neither white nor Indian fully grasped the concept of the other. The Indian wanted to live not just in the world, but with it; the white man, who thought in terms of estates and baronies, wanted land he alone could cultivate and use.

In the beginning, friendship and cooperation with the Indians were essential if the colonists were to gain a foothold in America, for the white man was badly outnumbered. To be unneighborly was to risk violence, and respect for Indian rights was the better part of wisdom. The upright conduct of the first colonists in Massachusetts and Virginia drew generous response from powerful chiefs who helped the settlements survive.

Live and let live was the inevitable opening keynote, for muskets could neither cut trees nor keep the peace. In the meeting of alien worlds both Indians and whites had something to learn from each other, and if the newcomers borrowed the idea of a feast of thanksgiving from a harvest celebration of neighboring Indians, so much the better.

But the first phase ended quickly, and as stockades were completed and new colonists swelled the ranks of the invaders, conciliation became superfluous. As one historian put it, "The Indians were pressed remorselessly when their friendship became of less value than their land." In Virginia, the Indians watched with consternation and alarm as the white men planted tobacco, used up the soil, and every few years moved on to clear new fields. The planters took the Indians' land, first by cajolery and trade, then by force. So swiftly did events move that, within forty years of the founding of Jamestown, the mighty Powhatans were landless and in beggary at the edge of their former homes. Elsewhere the details were different, but white expansion followed the same general pattern.

The barrier of misunderstanding that arose when advancing whites encountered Indians was too high for either people to scale. Some weak and venal chiefs bargained away the rights of their people, but for most tribes the sale of large tracts to the settlers was not a solution to their problems, for they had no land to sell. The warrior chief, Tecumseh, stated the Indian philosophy of nearly all tribes with his reply to the demands of white buyers: "Sell the country? . . . Why not sell the air, the clouds, the great sea?"

To the Indian mind, even after two centuries of acquaintance with the whites, land belonged collectively to the people who used it. The notion of private ownership of land, of land as a commodity to be bought and sold, was still alien to their thinking, and tribe after tribe resisted the idea to the death. Land belonged, they said again and again—in the hills of New York, in the Pennsylvania Alleghenies, and in the Ohio Valley—to their ancestors whose bones were buried in it, to the present generation which used it, and to their children who would inherit it. "The land we live on, our fathers received from God," said the Iroquois Cornplanter to George Washington in 1790, "and they transmitted it to us, for our children, and we cannot part with it. . . . Where is the land on which our children and their children after them are to lie down?"

Had the Indians lacked leaders of integrity, or been less emotionally tied to their hills and valleys, a compromise might have been arranged, but life and land were so intertwined in the Indian scheme of existence that retreat meant surrender of self—and that was unthinkable.

Before the moments of climax came, weaker tribes in all parts of the country made peace, and some of the stronger ones delayed the inevitable by selling parts of their domain. There were fierce chiefs, too, who would not bargain; men repeating the defiance of Canasatego who, representing the Six Nations in Philadelphia in 1742, spoke with contempt of the money and goods acquired in exchange for land. They were gone in a day or an hour, he said, but land was "everlasting."

Yet to many another red man, the new goods had an irresistible allure. Contact with the higher technology of Europeans began to make most of what the Indians had known obsolete, and created needs which they could satisfy only by making increased demands upon the bank of the earth. Once seen, a musket became essential to an Indian warrior; and once an Indian woman had used a steel needle or a woven blanket, she could never again be satisfied with a bone awl or a skin robe. The white man was the only source of the new essentials, and the only way to get them was by trade for things the white man wanted—meat, beaver—and later and farther west, pemmican and buffalo robes. So the Indian, too, became a raider of the American earth, and at the same time was himself raided for his lands by the superior technology and increasingly superior numbers of the white man.

The settlers' demand for new territory was insatiable, and what money could not buy, muskets, deceit, and official ruthlessness could win. Worse, as the bloody thrust and counterthrust went on, hatreds deepened and demagogues argued for a "final" solution of the Indian problem. They coined a slogan that became the byword of the American frontier: "The only good Indian is a dead Indian."

In the westward push, new land became the key to progress, and Indian policy was guided solely by economic expediency. A spokesman for the Ottawa, Sioux, Iowa, Winnebago, and other tribes made this sad and unsuccessful appeal at the Council of Drummond Island in 1816: "The Master of Life has given us lands for the support of our men, women, and children. He has given us fish, deer, buffalo, and every kind of birds and animals for our use. . . . When the Master of Life, or Great Spirit, put us on this land, it was for the purpose of enjoying the use of the animals and fishes, but certain it was never intended that we should sell it or any part thereof which gives us wood, grass and everything."

He got his answer the following year when President James Monroe wrote: "The hunter or savage state requires a greater extent of territory to sustain it than is compatible with the progress and just claims of civilized life . . . and must yield to it."

There was a continent to be redeemed from the wilderness, and the Indians' way of life had to be sacrificed. Thus the policy of forced removal was established, and the Five Civilized Tribes were sent, with scant civility and, in the end, scant humanity, on a thousand-mile "trail of tears" to Oklahoma.

In its latter stages the land war moved into its cruelest phase in California, the Southwest, and the Upper Great Plains. Most of the California Indians were neither as warlike nor as land-conscious as the Eastern tribes. But even this did not spare them, and the most pitiless chapters of the struggle were written by frustrated gold-seekers who organized vigilante raids, killed helpless natives, and subsequently collected from the government for their deeds of slaughter.

After the Civil War the "clear the redskins out" policy approached its dramatic climax. The mounted Indians of the Upper Great Plains and the Apaches of the Southwest were fierce warriors who would not be cornered. It took regiments of trained cavalrymen over twenty years to drive them from their sacred hills and hunting grounds. Outarmed and outmanned, these warriors made fierce counterattacks, and our American pride was dealt a grim blow when the hundredth anniversary of the Declaration of Independence was interrupted by the news of the Custer massacre. The undeclared racial war did not end until the final tragic chapters were written in the Pyrrhic victory of Sitting Bull at the Little Bighorn, and in the last stands of Crazy Horse, Chief Joseph, and Geronimo.

With the final triumphs of the cavalry, and the uneasy settlement of tribes on reservations, the old slogans gradually disappeared, and the new conscience expressed itself in the saying, "It's cheaper to feed'em than to fight'em."

The 1887 Allotment Act, which broke up parts of some reservations and gave individual title to some Indians, further stripped away Indian rights by forcing unprepared tribesmen to deal with unscrupulous land swindlers.

With the passage of time and the steady attrition of old ideas and beliefs, we are at last, hopefully, entering a final phase of the Indian saga. The present generation of Indians accepts the system their fathers could not comprehend. The national government strives to provide the Indian people with adequate health and education programs and to aid them in developing the potential of their human and natural resources. As a singular gesture of atonement, which no civilized country has ever matched, the Congress has established a tribunal, the Indians Claims Commission, through which tribes may be compensated for losses suffered when their lands were forcibly taken from them.

After long years of peace, we now have an opportunity to measure the influence of the Indians and their culture on the American way of life. They have left with us much more than the magic of place names that identify our rivers and forests and cities and mountains. They have made a contribution to our agriculture and to a better understanding of how to live in harmony with the land.

It is ironical that today the conservation movement finds itself turning back to ancient Indian land ideas, to the Indian understanding that we are not outside of nature, but of it. From this wisdom we can learn how to conserve the best parts of our continent.

In recent decades we have slowly come back to some of the truths that the Indians knew from the beginning: that unborn generations have a claim on the land equal to our own; that men need to learn from nature, to keep an ear to the earth, and to replenish their spirits in frequent contacts with animals and wild land. And most important of all, we are recovering a sense of reverence for the land.

But the settlers found the Indians' continent too natural and too wild. Though within a generation that wildness would begin to convert some of their sons, and though reverence for the natural world and its forces would eventually sound in much of our literature, finding its prophets in Thoreau and Muir, those first Europeans, even while looking upon the New World with wonder and hope, were determined to subjugate it.

2
Roots of Environmental Decay

Human beings have been fouling the Earth for centuries. But recently they have become surpassingly efficient at making a mess of their habitat. At the very root of this problem are two intimately related historical causes. First, there is the fact that the number of human beings taxing the Earth's life-support system has been increasing rapidly and continues to grow at an unprecedented rate. It took well over a million years to reach the present world population of some three and a half billion people; at the current growth rate it will take less than forty years to add the next three and a half billion. Clearly, population growth and environmental deterioration are inseparable; the plague of population explosion is causing immeasurable and inexorable violence to the Earth.

The second major force underlying increased environmental abuse has been the spread of industrialization, which fosters and sustains excessive populations that overtax the limits of the environment. The industrial revolution, with its use of steam power and, later, electric power and fossil-fuel-burning internal combustion engines, vastly increased the ability to provide for physical wants and to support large urban populations. It is the industrialized society that requires enormous energy and fuel resources; it is the industrialized society that demands toxic fertilizers, pesticides, herbicides, and detergents; it is the industrialized society that makes a garbage disposal site of all the Earth. And the benefits of an industrial society in the form of added leisure time, good diet, public health facilities, greater mobility, and a thousand physical comforts further encourage population growth. The tremendous impact upon the environment of excessive numbers of people in an industrialized society is only now being fully recognized.

People have been aware of the possible consequences of population explosion for some time. As early as 1798 the Englishman Thomas Robert Malthus posed a straightforward thesis: the people of the world were increasing faster than the Earth's capacity to support them—shortage of food resources would act as "a strong and constantly operating check on population." Malthus's gloomy prediction that food shortages would check human increase failed to materialize. Since he wrote the words in the excerpt included in this section, the number of people in the world has increased some three times over and food production has generally grown apace. In underdeveloped countries, however, famine and starvation have been common, bringing misery without curtailing population growth. Was Malthus, therefore, merely a fuzzy-minded prophet of doom? Paul Ehrlich, Stanford biologist and ecology activist, would say no. Malthus had no way of knowing that in the succeeding two centuries there would be unimaginable technological breakthroughs that would result in highly advanced agricultural techniques and an adequate food supply in developed nations. But Malthus's idea was sound: if people continue to increase their numbers at an unchecked geometrical ratio they will eventually outstrip the Earth's life-support capacity, which at best can grow at an arithmetical rate. Ehrlich is a modern Malthusian—some would say he is a new alarmist prophet of doom—who believes that if population growth is allowed to continue at such a fantastic rate, disaster is inevitable.

The significant point is that the upsurge in population means an increase in the demands upon the environment. For example, there are about 5,500 Americans born each day. The average American can expect to live some 70 years and in that time will have individual needs requiring the environment to furnish 26 million gallons of water, 21,000 gallons of gasoline, five tons of meat, fourteen tons of milk products, ten tons of wheat, and sixteen tons of pulpwood in paper products. This average American will expect the environment to produce these things and countless others and to absorb tons of waste in return. In just one year Americans pile up 30 million tons of waste paper, seven million scrapped automobiles, 80 billion bottles and cans, and contribute a full third of all the air pollutants in the world. Obviously, the most highly industrialized people—though only a small percentage of the world population—have an ecological impact all out of proportion to their numbers. In short, Americans, who are increasing at an alarming rate along with the rest of the world, are placing incredible strains upon the Earth, and they threaten to overwhelm its finite life-support capacity. The tie between the upsurge in population and the increase in environmental pollution is unavoidable. Some people are now referring to it as one problem—"populution."

Americans in particular appear to have developed a spirit of wastefulness and violence toward the environment. This attitude seems to have grown out of the historic abundance of the frontier, and now that the frontier is closed and there are no fresh lands to conquer they may well be caught in a permanent ecological crisis of their own making.

No force in history can quite match the impact of industrialism upon human affairs. Prior to the nineteenth century, there had been a rather plodding application of scientific knowledge which was generally absorbed by society without catastrophic disruptions. Science and technology appeared to be the obedient servants of humanity. More recently science and technology have sundered such restraints as once bound them and the entire collective human life has been reshaped in response to industrialism. Barry Commoner, biologist-turned-iconoclast, notes that technology is responsible for the material base of the twentieth century but that it is really a monster in disguise. Commoner's message is that the material benefits that have come with industrialization and the application of scientific knowledge carry unwelcome by-products which do inexorable harm to the environment. As people approach the zenith of technological achievement they are faced with threats on every hand from radioactive waste, oil afloat in the seas, dangerous chemical pesticides and fertilizers, auto pollution, and the destructive by-products of an industrial age—garbage of a thousand disgusting kinds. Technology has even fostered the mutation of formerly benign insects and microbes into virulent new threats to our well-being. Commoner warns that we are the victims of technological "advance": "we already know the enormous benefits it can bestow; we have begun to perceive its frightful threats." He calls upon scientists to discipline themselves and the society in order to avoid environmental catastrophe.

Commoner's alarm about the impact of industrialism and science upon the environment is shared by Britain's Lord Ritchie-Calder, who in the final selection in this section ties together the historical roots of the environmental crisis. Ritchie-Calder's primary concern is that people are frighteningly ignorant of the consequences of the application of technology to the environment. Science applied to agriculture has increased productivity; it has also created a threat to the fertility of the soil and to plant, animal, and human life through pesticide poisoning and by forcing pests to evolve into more resistant forms. Through scientific application people have learned to produce power on a fantastic scale; they have also begun to drain the Earth's resources and now threaten life through such agencies as thermal discharge and atomic waste. Science has helped cause the population explosion through otherwise laudable innovations, such as public health programs, sanitary engineering, and the widespread use of DDT and wonder drugs like penicillin, all of which reduce the death rate. Ritchie-Calder finds that the historic loyalty to science is misplaced. He agrees with Malthus and Ehrlich that runaway population growth is threatening to overwhelm the Earth's resources, and he echoes Commoner in his indictment of scientists who seem willing to race ahead with the application of technology while ignoring its impact on the biosphere.

Thomas Robert Malthus

On the Principle
of Population

I think I may fairly make two postulata.

First, That food is necessary to the existence of man.

Secondly, That the passion between the sexes is necessary, and will remain nearly in its present state.

These two laws ever since we have had any knowledge of mankind, appear to have been fixed laws of our nature; and, as we have not hitherto seen any alteration in them, we have no right to conclude that they will ever cease to be what they now are, without an immediate act of power in that Being who first arranged the system of the universe; and for the advantage of his creatures, still executes, according to fixed laws, all its various operations. . . .

Assuming then, my postulata as granted, I say, that the power of population is indefinitely greater than the power in the earth to produce subsistence for man.

Population, when unchecked, increases in a geometrical ratio. Subsistence increases only in an arithmetical ratio. A slight acquaintance with numbers will shew the immensity of the first power in comparison of the second.

By that law of our nature which makes food necessary to the life of man, the effects of these two unequal powers must be kept equal.

This implies a strong and constantly operating check on population from the difficulty of subsistence. This difficulty must fall some where; and must necessarily be severely felt by a large portion of mankind.

Through the animal and vegetable kingdoms, nature has scattered the seeds of life abroad with the most profuse and liberal hand. She has been comparatively sparing in the room, and the nourishment necessary to rear them. The germs of existence contained in this spot of earth, with ample food, and ample room to expand in, would fill millions of worlds in the course of a few thousand years. Necessity, that imperious all pervading law of nature, restrains them within the prescribed bounds. The race of plants, and the race of animals shrink under this great restrictive law. And the race of man cannot, by any efforts of reason, escape from it. Among plants and animals its effects are waste of seed, sickness, and premature death. Among mankind, misery and vice. The former, misery, is an absolutely necessary consequence of it. Vice is a highly probable consequence, and we therefore see it abundantly prevail; but it ought not, perhaps, to be called an absolutely necessary consequence. The ordeal of virtue is to resist all temptation to evil.

From "First Essay on Population" by Thomas Robert Malthus, 1798.

This natural inequality of the two powers of population, and of production in the earth, and that great law of our nature which must constantly keep their effects equal, form the great difficulty that to me appears insurmountable in the way to the perfectibility of society. All other arguments are of slight and subordinate consideration in comparison of this. I see no way by which man can escape from the weight of this law which pervades all animated nature. No fancied equality, no agrarian regulations in their utmost extent, could remove the pressure of it even for a single century. And it appears, therefore, to be decisive against the possible existence of a society, all the members of which, should live in ease, happiness, and comparative leisure; and feel no anxiety about providing the means of subsistence for themselves and families.

Consequently, if the premises are just, the argument is conclusive against the perfectibility of the mass of mankind.

Paul R. Ehrlich

The Population Bomb

I have understood the population explosion intellectually for a long time. I came to understand it emotionally one stinking hot night in Delhi a couple of years ago. My wife and daughter and I were returning to our hotel in an ancient taxi. The seats were hopping with fleas. The only functional gear was third. As we crawled through the city, we entered a crowded slum area. The temperature was well over 100, and the air was a haze of dust and smoke. The streets seemed alive with people. People eating, people washing, people sleeping. People visiting, arguing, and screaming. People thrusting their hands through the taxi window, begging. People defecating and urinating. People clinging to buses. People herding animals. People, people, people, people. As we moved slowly through the mob, hand horn squawking, the dust, noise, heat, and cooking fires gave the scene a hellish aspect. Would we ever get to our hotel? All three of us were, frankly, frightened. It seemed that anything could happen—but, of course, nothing did. Old India hands will laugh at our reaction. We were just some overprivileged tourists, unaccustomed to the sights and sounds of India. Perhaps, but since that night I've known the *feel* of overpopulation.

TOO MANY PEOPLE

Americans are beginning to realize that the undeveloped countries of the world face an inevitable population-food crisis. Each year food production in undeveloped countries falls a bit further behind burgeoning population growth, and people go to bed a little bit hungrier. While there are temporary or local reversals of this trend, it now seems inevitable that it will continue to its logical conclusion: mass starvation. The rich are going to get richer, but the more numerous poor are going to get poorer. Of these poor, a minimum of three and one-half million will starve to death this year, mostly children. But this is a mere handful compared to the numbers that will be starving in a decade or so. And it is now too late to take action to save many of those people.

In a book about population there is a temptation to stun the reader with an avalanche of statistics. I'll spare you most, but not all, of that. After all, no matter how you slice it, population is a numbers game. Perhaps the best way to impress you with numbers is to tell you about the "doubling time"—the time necessary for the population to double in size.

It has been estimated that the human population of 6000 B.C. was about five million people, taking perhaps one million years to get there from two and a half million. The population did not reach 500 million until almost 8,000 years later —about 1650 A.D. This means it doubled roughly once every thousand years or so. It reached a billion people around 1850, doubling in some 200 years. It took only 80 years or so for the next doubling, as the population reached two billion around 1930. We have not completed the next doubling to four billion yet, but we now have well over three billion people. The doubling time at present seems to be about 37 years. Quite a reduction in doubling times: 1,000,000 years, 1,000 years, 200 years, 80 years, 37 years. Perhaps the meaning of a doubling time of around 37 years is best brought home by a theoretical exercise. Let's examine what might happen on the absurd assumption that the population continued to double every 37 years into the indefinite future.

If growth continued at that rate for about 900 years, there would be some 60,000,000,000,000,000 people on the face of the earth. Sixty million billion people. This is about 100 persons for each square yard of the Earth's surface, land and sea. A British physicist, J. H. Fremlin, guessed that such a multitude might be housed in a continuous 2,000-story building covering our entire planet. The upper 1,000 stories would contain only the apparatus for running this gigantic warren. Ducts, pipes, wires, elevator shafts, etc., would occupy about half of the space in the bottom 1,000 stories. This would leave three or four yards of floor space for each person. I will leave to your imagination the physical details of existence in this ant heap, except to point out that all would not be black. Probably each person would be limited in his travel. Perhaps he could take elevators through all 1,000 residential stories but could travel only within a circle of a few hundred yards' radius on any floor. This would permit, however, each person to choose his friends from among some ten million people! And, as Fremlin points out, entertainment on the worldwide TV should be excellent, for at any time "one could expect some ten million Shakespeares and rather more Beatles to be alive."

Could growth of the human population of the Earth continue beyond that point? Not according to Fremlin. We would have reached a "heat limit." People themselves, as well as their activities, convert other forms of energy into heat which must be dissipated. In order to permit this excess heat to radiate directly from the top of the "world building" directly into space, the atmosphere would have been pumped into flasks under the sea well before the limiting population size was reached. The precise limit would depend on the technology of the day. At a population size of one billion billion people, the temperature of the "world roof" would be kept around the melting point of iron to radiate away the human heat generated.

But, you say, surely Science (with a capital "S") will find a way for us to occupy the other planets of our solar system and eventually of other stars before we get all that crowded. Skip for a moment the virtual certainty that those planets are uninhabitable. Forget also the insurmountable logistic problems of moving billions of people off the Earth. Fremlin has made some interesting calculations on how much time we could buy by occupying the planets of the solar system. For instance, at any given time it would take only about 50 years to populate Venus, Mercury, Mars, the moon, and the moons of Jupiter and Saturn to the same population density as Earth.

What if the fantastic problems of reaching and colonizing the other planets of the solar system, such as Jupiter and Uranus, can be solved? It would take only about 200 years to fill them "Earth-full." So we could perhaps gain 250 years of time for population growth in the solar system after we had reached an absolute limit on Earth. What then? We can't ship our surplus to the stars. Professor Garrett Hardin of the University of California at Santa Barbara has dealt effectively with this fantasy. Using extremely optimistic assumptions, he has calculated that Americans, by cutting their standard of living down to 18% of its present level, could in *one year* set aside enough capital to finance the exportation to the stars of *one day's* increase in the population of the world.

Interstellar transport for surplus people presents an amusing prospect. Since the ships would take generations to reach most stars, the only people who could be transported would be those willing to exercise strict birth control. Population explosions on space ships would be disastrous. Thus we would have to export our responsible people, leaving the irresponsible at home on Earth to breed.

Enough of fantasy. Hopefully, you are convinced that the population will have to stop growing sooner or later and that the extremely remote possibility of expanding into outer space offers no escape from the laws of population growth. If you still want to hope for the stars, just remember that, at the current growth rate, in a few thousand years everything in the visible universe would be converted into people, and the ball of people would be expanding with the speed of light! Unfortunately, even 900 years is much too far in the future for those of us concerned with the population explosion. [Evidence indicates that] the next *nine* years will probably tell the story.

Of course, population growth is not occurring uniformly over the face of the Earth. Indeed, countries are divided rather neatly into two groups: those with rapid growth rates, and those with relatively slow growth rates. The first group, making up about two-thirds of the world population, coincides closely with what are known as the "undeveloped countries" (UDCs). The UDCs are not industrialized, tend to have inefficient agriculture, very small gross national products, high illiteracy rates and related problems. That's what UDCs are technically, but a short definition of undeveloped is "starving." Most Latin American, African, and Asian countries fall into this category. The second group consists, in essence, of the "developed countries" (DCs). DCs are modern, industrial nations, such as the United States, Canada, most European countries, Israel, Russia, Japan, and Australia. Most people in these countries are adequately nourished.

Doubling times in the UDCs range around 20 to 35 years. Examples of these times (from the 1968 figures . . . released by the Population Reference Bureau) are Kenya, 24 years; Nigeria, 28; Turkey, 24; Indonesia, 31; Philippines, 20; Brazil, 22; Costa Rica, 20; and El Salvador, 19. Think of what it means for the population of a country to double in 25 years. In order just to keep living standards at the present inadequate level, the food available for the people must be doubled. Every structure and road must be duplicated. The amount of power must be doubled. The capacity of the transport system must be doubled. The number of trained doctors, nurses, teachers, and administrators must be doubled. This would be a fantastically difficult job in the United States—a rich country with a fine agricultural system, immense industries, and rich natural resources. Think of what it means to a country with none of these.

Remember also that in virtually all UDCs, people have gotten the word about the better life it is possible to have. They have seen colored pictures in magazines of the miracles of Western technology. They have seen automobiles and airplanes. They have seen American and European movies. Many have seen refrigerators, tractors, and even TV sets. Almost all have heard transistor radios. They *know* that a better life is possible. They have what we like to call "rising expectations." If twice as many people are to be happy, the miracle of doubling what they now have will not be enough. It will only maintain today's standard of living. There will have to be a tripling or better. Needless to say, they are not going to be happy.

Doubling times for the populations of the DCs tend to be in the 50-to-200-year range. Examples of 1968 doubling times are the United States, 63 years; Austria, 175; Denmark, 88; Norway, 88; United Kingdom, 140; Poland, 88; Russia, 63; Italy, 117; Spain, 88; and Japan, 63. These are industrialized countries that have undergone the so-called demographic transition—a transition from high to low growth rate. As industrialization progressed, children became less important to parents as extra hands to work on the farm and as support in old age. At the same time they became a financial drag—expensive to raise and educate. Presumably these are the reasons for a slowing of population growth after industrialization. They boil down to a simple fact—people just want to have fewer children.

This is not to say, however, that population is not a problem for the DCs.

First of all, most of them are overpopulated. They are overpopulated by the simple criterion that they are not able to produce enough food to feed their populations. It is true that they have the money to buy food, but when food is no longer available for sale they will find the money rather indigestible. Then, too, they share with the UDCs a serious problem of population distribution. Their urban centers are getting more and more crowded relative to the countryside. This problem is not as severe as it is in the UDCs (if current trends should continue, which they cannot, Calcutta could have 66 million inhabitants in the year 2000). As you are well aware, however, urban concentrations are creating serious problems even in America. In the United States, one of the more rapidly growing DCs, we hear constantly of the headaches caused by growing population: not just garbage in our environment, but overcrowded highways, burgeoning slums, deteriorating school systems, rising crime rates, riots, and other related problems.

From the point of view of a demographer, the whole problem is quite simple. A population will continue to grow as long as the birth rate exceeds the death rate— if immigration and emigration are not occurring. It is, of course, the balance between birth rate and death rate that is critical. The birth rate is the number of births per thousand people per year in the population. The death rate is the number of deaths per thousand people per year. Subtracting the death rate from the birth rate, and ignoring migration, gives the rate of increase. If the birth rate is 30 per thousand per year, and the death rate is 10 per thousand per year, then the rate of increase is 20 per thousand per year (30 - 10 = 20). Expressed as a percent (rate per hundred people), the rate of 20 per thousand becomes 2%. If the rate of increase is 2%, then the doubling time will be 35 years. Note that if you simply added 20 people per thousand per year to the population, it would take 50 years to add a second thousand people (20 × 50 = 1,000). But the doubling time is actually much less because populations grow at compound interest rates. Just as interest dollars themselves earn interest, so people added to populations produce more people. It's growing at compound interest that makes populations double so much more rapidly than seems possible. Look at the relationship between the annual percent increase (interest rate) and the doubling time of the population (time for your money to double):

Annual percent increase	Doubling time
1.0	70
2.0	35
3.0	24
4.0	17

Those are all the calculations—I promise. If you are interested in more details on how demographic figuring is done, you may enjoy reading Thompson and Lewis's excellent book, *Population Problems.*

There are some professional optimists around who like to greet every sign of dropping birth rates with wild pronouncements about the end of the population explosion. They are a little like a person who, after a low temperature of five below zero on December 21, interprets a low of only three below zero on December 22 as a cheery sign of approaching spring. First of all, birth rates, along with all demographic statistics, show short-term fluctuations caused by many factors. For instance, the birth rate depends rather heavily on the number of women at reproductive age. In the United States the current low birth rates soon will be replaced by higher rates as more post World War II "baby boom" children move into their reproductive years. In Japan, 1966, the Year of the Fire Horse, was a year of very low birth rates. There is widespread belief that girls born in the Year of the Fire Horse make poor wives, and Japanese couples try to avoid giving birth in that year because they are afraid of having daughters.

But, I repeat, it is the relationship between birth rate and death rate that is most critical. Indonesia, Laos, and Haiti all had birth rates around 46 per thousand in 1966. Costa Rica's birth rate was 41 per thousand. Good for Costa Rica? Unfortunately, not very. Costa Rica's death rate was less than nine per thousand, while the other countries all had death rates above 20 per thousand. The population of Costa Rica in 1966 was doubling every 17 years, while the doubling times of Indonesia, Laos, and Haiti were all above 30 years. Ah, but, you say, it was good for Costa Rica—fewer people per thousand were dying each year. Fine for a few years perhaps, but what then? Some 50% of the people in Costa Rica are under 15 years old. As they get older, they will need more and more food in a world with less and less. In 1983 they will have twice as many mouths to feed as they had in 1966, if the 1966 trend continues. Where will the food come from? Today the death rate in Costa Rica is low in part because they have a large number of physicians in proportion to their population. How do you suppose those physicians will keep the death rate down when there's not enough food to keep people alive?

One of the most ominous facts of the current situation is that roughly 40% of the population of the undeveloped world is made up of people *under 15 years old.* As that mass of young people moves into its reproductive years during the next decade, we're going to see the greatest baby boom of all time. Those youngsters are the reason for all the ominous predictions for the year 2000. They are the gunpowder for the population explosion.

How did we get into this bind? It all happened a long time ago, and the story involves the process of natural selection, the development of culture, and man's swollen head. The essence of success in evolution is reproduction. Indeed, natural selection is simply defined as differential reproduction of genetic types. That is, if people with blue eyes have more children on the average than those with brown eyes, natural selection is occurring. More genes for blue eyes will be passed on to the next generation than will genes for brown eyes. Should this continue, the population will have progressively larger and larger proportions of blue-eyed people. This differential reproduction of genetic types is the driving force of evolution; it has been driving evolution for billions of years. Whatever types produced more offspring became the common types. Virtually all populations contain very many different genetic types (for reasons that need not concern us), and some are always outreproducing others. As I said, reproduction is the key to winning the evolutionary game. Any structure, physiological process, or pattern of behavior that leads to greater reproductive success will tend to be perpetuated. The entire process by which man developed involves thousands of millennia of our ancestors being more successful breeders than their relatives. Facet number one of our bind—the urge to reproduce has been fixed in us by billions of years of evolution.

Of course through all those years of evolution, our ancestors were fighting a continual battle to keep the birth rate ahead of the death rate. That they were successful is attested to by our very existence, for, if the death rate had overtaken the birth rate for any substantial period of time, the evolutionary line leading to man would have gone extinct. Among our apelike ancestors, a few million years ago, it was still very difficult for a mother to rear her children successfully. Most of the offspring died before they reached reproductive age. The death rate was near the birth rate. Then another factor entered the picture—cultural evolution was added to biological evolution.

Culture can be loosely defined as the body of nongenetic information which people pass from generation to generation. It is the accumulated knowledge that, in the old days, was passed on entirely by word of mouth, painting, and demonstration. Several thousand years ago the written word was added to the means of cultural transmission. Today culture is passed on in these ways, and also through television, computer tapes, motion pictures, records, blueprints, and other media. Culture is all the information man possesses except for that which is stored in the chemical language of his genes.

The large size of the human brain evolved in response to the development of cultural information. A big brain is an advantage when dealing with such information. Big-brained individuals were able to deal more successfully with the culture of their group. They were thus more successful reproductively than their smaller-brained relatives. They passed on their genes for big brains to their numerous offspring. They also added to the accumulating store of cultural information, increasing slightly the premium placed on brain size in the next generation. A self-reinforcing selective trend developed—a trend toward increased brain size.

But there was, quite literally, a rub. Babies had bigger and bigger heads. There were limits to how large a woman's pelvis could conveniently become. To make a long story short, the strategy of evolution was not to make a woman bell-shaped and relatively immobile, but to accept the problem of having babies who were helpless for a long period while their brains grew after birth. How could the mother defend and care for her infant during its unusually long period of helplessness? She couldn't, unless Papa hung around. The girls are still working on that problem, but an essential step was to get rid of the short, well-defined breeding season characteristic of most mammals. The year-round sexuality of the human female, the long period of infant dependence on the female, the evolution of the family group, all are at the roots of our present problem. They are essential ingredients in the vast social phenomenon that we call sex. Sex is not simply an act leading to the production of offspring. It is a varied and complex cultural phenomenon penetrating into all aspects of our lives—one involving our self-esteem, our choice of friends, cars, and leaders. It is tightly interwoven with our mythologies and history. Sex in man is necessary for the production of young, but it also evolved to ensure their successful rearing. Facet number two of our bind—our urge to reproduce is hopelessly entwined with most of our other urges.

Of course, in the early days the whole system did not prevent a very high mortality among the young, as well as among the older members of the group. Hunting and food-gathering is a risky business. Cavemen had to throw very impressive cave bears out of their caves before the men could move in. Witch doctors and shamans had a less than perfect record at treating wounds and curing disease. Life was short, if not sweet. Man's total population size doubtless increased slowly but steadily as human populations expanded out of the African cradle of our species.

Then about 8,000 years ago a major change occurred—the agricultural revolution. People began to give up hunting food and settled down to grow it. Suddenly some of the risk was removed from life. The chances of dying of starvation diminished greatly in some human groups. Other threats associated with the nomadic life were also reduced, perhaps balanced by new threats of disease and large-scale warfare associated with the development of cities. But the overall result was a more secure existence than before, and the human population grew more rapidly. Around 1800, when the standard of living in what are today the DCs was dramatically increasing due to industrialization, population growth really began to accelerate. The development of medical science was the straw that broke the camel's back. While lowering death rates in the DCs was due in part to other factors, there is no question that "instant death control," exported by the DCs, has been responsible for the drastic lowering of death rates in the UDCs. Medical science, with its efficient public health programs, has been able to depress the death rate with astonishing rapidity and at the same time drastically increase the birth rate; healthier people have more babies.

The power of exported death control can best be seen by an examination of the classic case of Ceylon's assault on malaria after World War II. Between 1933 and 1942 the death rate due directly to malaria was *reported* as almost two per thousand. This rate, however, represented only a portion of the malaria deaths, as many were reported as being due to "pyrexia." Indeed, in 1934-1935 a malaria epidemic may have been directly responsible for fully half of the deaths on the island. In addition, malaria, which infected a large portion of the population, made people susceptible to many other diseases. It thus contributed to the death rate indirectly as well as directly.

The introduction of DDT in 1946 brought rapid control over the mosquitoes which carry malaria. As a result, the death rate on the island was halved in less than a decade. The death rate in Ceylon in 1945 was 22. It dropped 34% between 1946 and 1947 and moved down to ten in 1954. Since the sharp postwar drop it has continued to decline and how stands at eight. Although part of the drop is doubtless due to the killing of other insects which carry disease and to other public health measures, most of it can be accounted for by the control of malaria.

Victory over malaria, yellow fever, smallpox, cholera, and other infectious diseases has been responsible for similar plunges in death rate throughout most of the UDCs. In the decade 1940-1950 the death rate declined 46% in Puerto Rico, 43% in Formosa, and 23% in Jamaica. In a sample of 18 undeveloped areas the average decline in death rate between 1945 and 1950 was 24%.

It is, of course, socially very acceptable to reduce the death rate. Billions of years of evolution have given us all a powerful will to live. Intervening in the birth rate goes against our evolutionary values. During all those centuries of our evolutionary past, the individuals who had the most children passed on their genetic endowment in greater quantities than those who reproduced less. Their genes dominate our heredity today. All our biological urges are for more reproduction, and they are all too often reinforced by our culture. In brief, death control goes with the grain, birth control against it.

In summary, the world's population will continue to grow as long as the birth rate exceeds the death rate; it's as simple as that. When it stops growing or starts to shrink, it will mean that either the birth rate has gone down or the death rate has gone up or a combination of the two. Basically, then, there are only two kinds of solutions to the population problem. One is a "birth rate solution," in which we find ways to lower the birth rate. The other is a "death rate solution," in which ways to raise the death rate—war, famine, pestilence—*find us.* The problem could have been avoided by *population control,* in which mankind consciously adjusted the birth rate so that a "death rate solution" did not have to occur.

Barry Commoner

Sorcerer's Apprentice

We are surrounded by the technological successes of science: space vehicles, nuclear power, new synthetic chemicals, medical advances that increase the length and usefulness of human life. But we also see some sharp contrasts. While one group of scientists studies ways to provide air for the first human visitors to the moon, another tries to learn why we are fouling the air that the rest of us must breathe on earth. We hear of masterful schemes for using nuclear explosions to extract pure water from the moon; but in some American cities the water that flows from the tap is undrinkable and the householder must buy drinking water in bottles. Science is triumphant with far-ranging success, but its triumph is somehow clouded by growing difficulties in providing for the simple necessities of human life on the earth.

OUR POLLUTED ENVIRONMENT

For about a million years human beings have survived and proliferated on the earth by fitting unobtrusively into a life-sustaining environment, joining a vast community in which animals, plants, microorganisms, soil, water, and air are tied together in an elaborate network of mutual relationships. In the preindustrial world the environment appeared to hold an unlimited store of clean air and water. It seemed reasonable, as the need arose, to vent smoke into the sky and sewage into rivers in the expectation that the huge reserves of uncontaminated air and water would effectively dilute and degrade the pollutants—perhaps in the same optimistic spirit that leads us to embed slotted boxes in bathroom walls to receive razor blades. But there is simply not enough air and water on the earth to absorb current man-made wastes without effect. We have begun to merit the truculent complaint against the works of the paleface voiced by Chief Satinpenny in Nathanael West's *A Cool Million:* "Now even the Grand Canyon will no longer hold razor blades."

Fire, an ancient friend, has become a man-made threat to the environment through the sheer quantity of the waste it produces. Each ton of wood, coal, petroleum, or natural gas burned contributes several tons of carbon dioxide to the earth's atmosphere. Between 1860 and 1960 the combustion of fuels added nearly 14 percent to the carbon-dioxide content of the air, which had until then remained constant for many centuries. Carbon dioxide plays an important role in regulating the temperature of the earth because of the "greenhouse effect." Both glass and carbon dioxide tend to pass visible light but absorb infrared rays. This explains why the sun so easily warms a greenhouse on a winter day. Light from the sun enters through the greenhouse glass. Within, it is absorbed by soil and plants and converted to infrared heat energy which remains trapped inside the greenhouse because it cannot pass out again through the glass. Carbon dioxide makes a huge greenhouse of the earth, allowing sunlight to reach the earth's surface but limiting reradiation of the resulting heat into space. The temperature of the earth—which profoundly affects the suitability of the environment for life—is therefore certain to rise as the amount of carbon dioxide in the air increases.

A report by the President's Science Advisory Committee finds that the extra heat due to fuel-produced carbon dioxide accumulated in the air by the year 2000 might be sufficient to melt the Antarctic ice cap—in 4000 years according to one computation, or in 400 years according to another. And the report states: "The melting of the Antarctic ice cap would raise sea level by 400 feet. If 1,000 years were required to melt the ice cap, the sea level would rise about 4 feet every 10 years, 40 feet per century." This would result in catastrophe for much of the world's inhabited land and many of its major cities.

A more recent energy source—the internal-combustion engine—is polluting the environment much faster than fire. The automobile is only about seventy years old, but in that time it has severly damaged the quality of the air. The air over most large cities carries a large burden of waste automobile fuel. On exposure to sunlight this forms the noxious ingredients of smog, which significantly increases the incidence of respiratory disease. Since tetraethyl lead was introduced in 1923 as an automobile fuel additive, lead has contaminated most of the earth's surface. Increasing amounts of the metal are found in surface ocean waters, in crops, and in human blood, in which in some areas the amount may be approaching toxic levels.

As large a body of water as Lake Erie has already been overwhelmed by pollutants and has, in effect, died. In its natural state, Lake Erie was a balanced system in which water plants, microorganisms, and a great variety of swimming creatures lived together in an intricate harmony. But today most of Lake Erie is dead. Sewage, industrial wastes, and the runoff from heavily fertilized farmlands have loaded the waters of the lake with so much excess phosphate and nitrate as to jar the biology of the lake permanently out of balance. The fish are all but gone. According to a recent report by a committee of the National Academy of Sciences, within about twenty years city wastes are expected to overwhelm the biology of most of the nation's waterways.

Small amounts of nitrate are naturally present in all bodies of water, and living things can tolerate—and often require—nitrate at these low levels. Now, however, nitrate originating in the outflow waters of sewage-treatment plants and in the runoff from land treated with chemical fertilizers has begun to build up excessively in ground water in thirty-eight regions of the United States, according to a recent Geological Survey report. Excess nitrate is poisonous to man and animals. About 8 to 9 parts per million of nitrate in drinking water causes a serious respiratory difficulty in infants—cyanosis—by interfering with hemoglobin function. For domestic animals 5 parts per million is considered unsafe. Some wells in the United States already have more than 3 parts per million of nitrate, and the contamination levels will go up with increased use of fertilizers and the growing density of population.

Added to the growing volume of the more familiar wastes are numerous new pollutants, produced through the ingenuity of modern physics and chemistry: radioactive elements, detergents, pesticides, weed killers, and a variety of industrial wastes. The greatest single source of contamination of the planet is now the radioactivity from test explosions of nuclear weapons in the atmosphere. Fallout from nuclear tests contaminates every part of the earth's surface and all of its inhabitants. Strontium-90, one of the radioactive constituents of fallout, is being built into the bones of every living person and will be carried in the bodies of several future generations. The fallout problem can tell us a good deal about the connection between modern science and the hazards of life on the earth.

Contamination of the earth's surface with fallout originates in the scientific revolution set off fifty years ago by far-reaching discoveries in atomic physics. By 1940 it was apparent that the new knowledge of atomic structure could lead to technological processes of vast power and scope. That these potentialities were so rapidly realized reflects the force of military demands. Faced with the grim dangers of war with Nazi Germany, the governments of the United States and Great Britain undertook the monumental task of translating what was until then an esoteric laboratory experiment—nuclear fission—into the awesome reality of the nuclear bomb. The bomb was created by the magnificent new insights of nuclear physics, driven to success by the determination to apply the full force of modern science to victory in the war.

With later scientific advances, nuclear weapons of increasing explosive power became possible. Propelled by the fears and tension of the cold war, these possibilities were fully exploited by those nations capable of making the necessary economic and technological effort—the United States, the U.S.S.R., Great Britain, and to a lesser extent, France and China. As a result, in 1948 there began a constantly accelerating series of nuclear explosions designed to develop weapons of increasing destructiveness and versatility. The total explosive power released by nuclear-weapon tests between 1948 and 1962 was equivalent to about 500 million tons of TNT—nearly two hundred times the total power of all the bombs dropped on Germany in World War II. The amount of only one fallout component—strontium-90—released by nuclear tests has introduced into the environment radioactivity equivalent to about 1 billion grams of radium. The significance of this sudden radioactive intrusion can be visualized by comparing it with the world supply of radium before World War II—about 10 grams. Until the advent of nuclear fission these few grams of radium represented the total human experience in handling radioactive substances.

The rapid and unchecked expansion of nuclear weaponry, which now dominates the world's major military programs, testifies to the enormous success of nuclear physics and engineering. There have been no complaints about the power and reliability of nuclear weapons. But official appraisals of the *biological* consequences of nuclear explosions have undergone a drastic change. Contrast statements, only eight years apart, by two American presidents:

President Eisenhower, October 1956: "The continuance of the present rate of H-bomb testing, by the most sober and responsible scientific judgment . . . does not imperil the health of humanity."

President Johnson, October 1964: "This treaty [the nuclear test-ban treaty] has halted the steady, menacing increase of radioactive fallout. The deadly products of atomic explosions were poisoning our soil and our food and the milk our children drank and the air we all breathe. Radioactive deposits were being formed in increasing quantity in the teeth and bones of young Americans. Radioactive poisons were beginning to threaten the safety of people throughout the world. They were a growing menace to the health of every unborn child."

There were, of course, some political reasons for this dramatic reversal in government policy—even President Eisenhower softened his rejection of the nuclear test ban before he left office. But it is now quite clear from available documents that between 1956 and 1963, when the U.S.-Soviet nuclear-test-ban treaty was signed, there were also sharp revisions in our appraisal of the fallout hazard.

Evaluation of this problem calls for a detailed analysis of the passage of radioactive isotopes—for example, strontium-90—from their creation in the nuclear fireball to their entry into the human body. When formed, strontium-90 and other radioactive elements become attached to tiny dustlike particles. These are shot high into the stratosphere by the explosion and return to earth at a rate which depends on the size of the particle and on the weather. Eventually the fallout is carried to the earth in rain or snow. From that point its fate is determined by the complex biology of soil, plants, domestic animals, and finally man. For example, since strontium-90 is a chemical relative of calcium, it takes a similar biological course. Along with calcium and other minerals, strontium-90 enters grass and crop plants through their roots and from raindrops resting on their leaves. When cows eat the contaminated grass the strontium-90 concentrates in their milk, which is rich in calcium. People absorb strontium-90 from contaminated milk and other foods. Once the amount of fallout absorbed in the body is known, its radiation output can be calculated and the resultant medical risk of radiation-induced cancer or genetic change can be estimated. . . .

In one sense the nuclear test program must be regarded as a remarkable scientific triumph, for it solved very difficult physics and engineering problems. But the biological consequences of the nuclear test program—the vast intrusion of radioactivity into animals, plants, and man—must be regarded as a huge technological mistake. There have been serious oversights and miscalculations. It is now clear that the government agencies responsible for the development of nuclear weapons embarked on this massive program before they understood the full biological effects of what they proposed to do. Great amounts of fallout were disseminated throughout the world before it became known that the resultant medical risks were so great as to require that nuclear testing be halted. The enactment of the test-ban treaty in 1963 is, in part, a confession of this failure of modern science and technology.

DETERGENTS

A different kind of pact—an agreement among the companies that make up the multibillion-dollar United States detergent industry—was needed to correct another big technological mistake. These companies agreed to replace, by July 1, 1965, the main active ingredient which, beginning in the early 1940s, had enabled their products to capture the major share of the cleanser market.

Detergents are chemicals, synthesized from raw materials found in petroleum, which have largely replaced soap in many household and industrial uses. Soap is itself one of the earliest-known useful chemicals. Long ago, it was discovered that fats and oils extracted from animals or pressed from seeds, and cooked with alkali, react chemically to form soap. Soap is a double-headed molecule. Its fatty part readily combines with droplets of greasy dirt, forming a film around them. The other end of the molecule forms the outer layer of the soap-coated dirt particle and has a strong affinity for water. As a result, the whole complex can be washed away.

But soap has certain technical and economic disadvantages. In "hard" water, which has a high mineral content, soap forms a deposit which will not readily wash away. In addition, the raw material, fat, is dependent on agriculture, hence variable in quality, availability, and price.

In the 1930s chemical technology began to produce synthetic organic compounds which closely resemble natural products: synthetic fibers, plastics, and artificial rubber. The inadequacies of soap were an attractive challenge for chemical engineers, who set out to make a synthetic washing agent that might avoid the hard-water problem and be independent of the vagaries of agriculture.

Detergent research began with fatlike molecules—hydrocarbons—which are common in petroleum. Chemists found ways to attach to the hydrocarbon a water-soluble molecular group containing sulfur. The result was a family of substances which, like soap, formed a water-soluble coat around grease particles. But the new detergents were better than soap, since they were equally effective in hard or soft water. Intensive research produced detergents with other useful properties: long shelf life; pleasantness to touch, sight, and smell; gentleness on the hands; economical price. This success illustrates the effectiveness of modern chemical research.

Within a few years after the new detergents were placed on sale, they had won a very large portion of the cleanser market. By 1960 they had replaced soap as the major household and industrial cleanser. A new billion-dollar industry had been created. However, one aspect of this technological triumph received no attention in the research laboratories—the effects of dumping a huge amount of new synthetic substances (about 3.5 billion pounds per year in the United States in 1960) down drains into waste-disposal systems. This lack of interest was perhaps natural, since the purchases of detergents—and the consequent profits—result from their effectiveness as cleansers and not from their behavior in waste systems. Finally it became difficult to ignore this aspect. Mounds of detergent foam appeared in riverways; in some places a glass of water drawn from a tap foamed up a head that would make a brewer envious. Only then was it discovered that, despite their useful similarities to soap, the new detergents differed from the natural product in one important way. When soap enters waste-disposal systems, it is readily broken down by bacteria, but the detergents are not. They pass through the waste system unchanged, appearing in the runoff water that drains into rivers, streams, and underground waters. Water supplies taken from these sources therefore contain detergents.

Now, for the first time, industrial chemists were forced to investigate another aspect of detergent chemistry: Why do detergents resist natural degradation? The difficulty was found to arise from the structure of the hydrocarbon skeleton of their molecules. Hydrocarbon molecules consist of a chain of carbon atoms, to each of which are attached two or three hydrogen atoms. The troublesome detergents had branched chains, and it was discovered that the bacterial enzymes which readily break up natural unbranched hydrocarbons in sewage plants are unable to degrade the synthetic branched hydrocarbons.

By the 1960s, water contamination had become bad enough to stimulate legislative action—and, simultaneously, the needed research. Resulting knowledge of the basic cause of the difficulty suggested a possible remedy. Methods were developed for producing degradable detergents from the unbranched hydrocarbon molecules that are also found in petroleum. The industry agreed to replace the branched-molecule detergents with branchless ones by July 1, 1965.

This solves part of the problem. In the large well-aerated sewage systems of most urban communities the new detergents are destroyed by bacteria. However, they do not break down as readily in underground unaerated systems, such as septic tanks. About 34 percent of the homes in the United States are equipped with septic systems. Since half of these also obtain water from their own wells, even the new "degradable" detergents may cause trouble. Moreover, when they are degraded the new synthetic detergents may overload surface waters with phosphate, leading to serious upsets in biological balance, such as the disaster which has already overtaken Lake Erie.

Thus, long after synthetic detergents had become a common household item, they were found to cause an intolerable nuisance in water supplies. There is no way to gloss over this episode. It represents a failure on the part of modern chemical technology to predict a vital consequence of a massive intervention into nature.

INSECTICIDES

My final example is one from personal experience. During World War II, I served as project officer in the Navy's development of aircraft dispersal of DDT, which proved to be of great importance in the Pacific island battles by protecting the first wave of attackers from serious insect-borne diseases. The project required meticulous studies of aerosol production, aerodynamic distribution of insecticide droplets, insect kill, meteorological effects, and the problems of flying tactics. Toward the end of our work, when the system was ready for fleet operations, we received a request for help from an experimental rocket station on a strip of island beach off the New Jersey coast. Flies were so numerous on the beach that important military developments were being held up. We sprayed the island and, inevitably, some of the surrounding waters with DDT. Within a few hours the flies were dead, and the rocketeers went about their work with renewed vigor. But a week later they were on the telephone again. A mysterious epidemic had littered the beach with tons of decaying fish—which had attracted vast swarms of flies from the mainland. This is how we learned that DDT kills fish.

Such unexpected twists are often encountered when new synthetic substances are thrust into the complex community of life: a wholly unanticipated development wipes out their original usefulness, or sometimes creates a problem worse than the original one. In one Bolivian town, DDT sprayed to control malarial mosquitoes also killed most of the local cats. With the cats gone, the village was invaded by a wild, mouselike animal that carried black typhus. Before new cats were brought to restore the balance, several hundred villagers were killed by the disease.

THE SCIENTIFIC BACKGROUND
OF TECHNOLOGICAL FAILURES

These problems have a common scientific background. Each of them springs from a useful technological innovation. The burning of fuel by internal-combustion engines is an enormously valuable source of energy—but also pollutes the air. New synthetic chemicals, the fruits of remarkable advances in chemical technology since World War II, appear in a multitude of useful forms—but also as new pollutants of air and water. The development, about twenty-five years ago, of self-sustained nuclear reactions has given us not only new weapons and new sources of power, but unprecedented radioactive debris as well.

Most of these problems seem to crop up unexpectedly. The sunlight-induced chemical conversion of airborne hydrocarbons (such as gasoline vapor) into smog was discovered, not in a chemical laboratory but in the air over Los Angeles, long after the chief mode for disseminating these hydrocarbons—the superhighway—was well entrenched in the urban economy. The full significance of the absorption of fallout into the human body became known only some years after the establishment of massive programs of nuclear testing. Most of the medical hazards of the new insecticides were noticed only long after these substances were in wide use. All these problems have been imposed on us—sometimes to our considerable surprise—well after the causative activity was in full swing.

Could we cure these difficulties by calling a halt to science and new technologies? The present accelerating growth of science and technology—which, together with population growth, is the cause of most of our pollution problems—was set in motion more than sixty years ago. Its roots are in the scientific revolution which took place at the turn of the century, when physicists discovered that the apparently simple laws of Newton's time concealed a complex world of exceedingly small particles and immense forces. From this knowledge has come the great flowering of modern science—including the new energy sources and synthetic substances which have covered the earth with pollution. We are today witnessing the inevitable impact of the tidal wave created by a scientific revolution more than half a century old. It is simply too late to declare a moratorium on the progress of science. . . .

To those of us who are concerned with the growing risk of unintended damage to the environment, some would reply that it is the grand purpose of science to move into unknown territory, to explore, and to discover. They would remind us that similar hazards have been risked before, and that science and technology cannot make progress without taking some risks. But the size and persistence of possible errors has also grown with the power of science and the expansion of technology. In the past, the risks taken in the name of technological progress—boiler explosions on the first steamboats, or the early injuries from radium—were restricted to a small place and a short time. The new hazards are neither local nor brief. Air pollution covers vast areas. Fallout is worldwide. Synthetic chemicals may remain in the soil for years. Radioactive pollutants now on the earth's surface will be found there for generations, and, in the case of carbon-14, for thousands of years. Excess carbon dioxide from fuel combustion eventually might cause floods that could cover much of the earth's present land surface for centuries. At the same time the permissible margin for error has become very much reduced. In the development of steam engines a certain number of boiler explosions were tolerated as the art was improved. If a single comparable disaster were to occur in a nuclear power plant or in a reactor-driven ship near a large city, thousands of people might die and a whole region be rendered uninhabitable—a price that the public might be unwilling to pay for nuclear power. The risk is one that private insurance companies have refused to underwrite. Modern science and technology are simply too powerful to permit a trial-and-error approach. . . .

As a biologist, I have reached this conclusion: we have come to a turning point in the human habitation of the earth. The environment is a complex, subtly balanced system, and it is this integrated whole which receives the impact of all the separate insults inflicted by pollutants. Never before in the history of this planet has its thin life-supporting surface been subjected to such diverse, novel, and potent agents. I believe that the cumulative effects of these pollutants, their interactions and amplification, can be fatal to the complex fabric of the biosphere. And, because man is, after all, a dependent part of this system, I believe that continued pollution of the earth, if unchecked, will eventually destroy the fitness of this planet as a place for human life. . . .

Technology has not only built the magnificent material base of modern society, but also confronts us with threats to survival which cannot be corrected unless we solve very grave economic, social, and political problems.

Lord Ritchie-Calder

Mortgaging the Old Homestead

Past civilizations are buried in the graveyards of their own mistakes, but as each died of its greed, its carelessness or its effeteness another took its place. That was because such civilizations took their character from a locality or region. Today ours is a global civilization; it is not bounded by the Tigris and the Euphrates nor even the Hellespont and the Indus; it is the whole world. Its planet has shrunk to a neighborhood round which a man-made satellite can patrol 16 times a day, riding

From "Mortgaging the Old Homestead" by Lord Ritchie-Calder. Reprinted by permission from *Foreign Affairs,* Vol. 48 (January 1970), pp. 207-220. Copyright © 1969 by the Council on Foreign Relations, Inc., New York.

the gravitational fences of Man's family estate. It is a community so interdependent that our mistakes are exaggerated on a world scale.

For the first time in history, Man has the power of veto over the evolution of his own species through a nuclear holocaust. The overkill is enough to wipe out every man, woman and child on earth, together with our fellow lodgers, the animals, the birds and the insects, and to reduce our planet to a radioactive wilderness. Or the Doomsday Machine could be replaced by the Doomsday Bug. By gene manipulation and man-made mutations, it is possible to produce, or generate, a disease against which there would be no natural immunity; by "generate" is meant that even if the perpetrators inoculated themselves protectively, the disease in spreading round the world could assume a virulence of its own and involve them, too. When a British bacteriologist died of the bug he had invented, a distinguished scientist said, "Thank God he didn't sneeze; he could have started a pandemic against which there would have been no immunity."

Modern Man can outboast the Ancients, who in the arrogance of their material achievements built pyramids as the gravestones of their civilizations. We can blast our pyramids into space to orbit through all eternity round a planet which perished by our neglect.

A hundred years ago Claude Bernard, the famous French physiologist, enjoined his colleagues, "True science teaches us to doubt and in ignorance to refrain." What he meant was that the scientist must proceed from one tested foothold to the next (like going into a minefield with a mine detector). Today we are using the biosphere, the living space, as an experimental laboratory. When the mad scientist of fiction blows himself and his laboratory skyhigh, that is all right, but when scientists and decision-makers act out of ignorance and pretend that it is knowledge, they are putting the whole world in hazard. Anyway, science at best is not wisdom; it is knowledge, while wisdom is knowledge tempered with judgment. Because of overspecialization, most scientists are disabled from exercising judgments beyond their own sphere.

A classic example was the atomic bomb. It was the Physicists' Bomb. When the device exploded at Alamogordo on July 16, 1945, and made a notch mark in history from which Man's future would be dated, the safe-breakers had cracked the lock of the nucleus before the locksmiths knew how it worked. (The evidence of this is the billions of dollars which have been spent since 1945 on gargantuan machines to study the fundamental particles, the components of the nucleus; and they still do not know how they interrelate.)

Prime Minister Clement Attlee, who concurred with President Truman's decision to drop the bomb on Hiroshima, later said: "We knew nothing whatever at that time about the genetic effects of an atomic explosion. I knew nothing about fallout and all the rest of what emerged after Hiroshima. As far as I know, President Truman and Winston Churchill knew nothing of those things either, nor did Sir John Anderson, who coordinated research on our side. Whether the scientists directly concerned knew or guessed, I do not know. But if they did, then so far as I am aware, they said nothing of it to those who had to make the decision."

That sounds absurd, since as long before as 1927, Herman J. Muller had been studying the genetic effects of radiation, work for which he was later awarded the Nobel Prize. But it is true that in the whole documentation of the British effort, before it merged in the Manhattan Project, there is only one reference to genetic effects—a Medical Research Council minute which was not connected with the bomb they were intending to make; it concerned the possibility that the Germans might, short of the bomb, produce radioactive isotopes as a form of biological warfare. In the Franck Report, the most statesmanlike document ever produced by scientists, with its percipience of the military and political consequences of unilateral use of the bomb (presented to Secretary of War Henry L. Stimson even before the test bomb exploded), no reference is made to the biological effects, although one would have supposed that to have been a very powerful argument. The explanation, of course, was that it was the Physicists' Bomb and military security restricted information and discussion to the bomb-makers, which excluded the biologists.

The same kind of breakdown in interdisciplinary consultation was manifest in the subsequent testing of fission and fusion bombs. Categorical assurances were given that the fallout would be confined to the testing area, but the Japanese fishing boat *Lucky Dragon* was "dusted" well outside the predicted range. Then we got the story of radiostrontium. Radiostrontium is an analog of calcium. Therefore in bone-formation an atom of natural strontium can take the place of calcium and the radioactive version can do likewise. For all practical purposes radiostrontium did not exist in the world before 1945; it is a man-made element. Today every young person, anywhere in the world, whose bones were forming during the massive bomb-testing in the atmosphere, carries this brand mark of the Atomic Age. The radiostrontium in their bones is medically insignificant, but, if the test ban (belated recognition) had not prevented the escalation of atmospheric testing, it might not have been.

Every young person everywhere was affected, and why? Because those responsible for H-bomb testing miscalculated. They assumed that the upthrust of the H-bomb would punch a hole in the stratosphere and that the gaseous radioactivity would dissipate itself. One of those gases was radioactive krypton, which quickly decays into radiostrontium, which is a particulate. The technicians had been wrongly briefed about the nature of the troposphere, the climatic ceiling which would, they maintained, prevent the fallback. But between the equatorial troposphere and the polar troposphere there is a gap, and the radiostrontium came back through this fanlight into the climatic jet streams. It was swept all round the world to come to earth as radioactive rain, to be deposited on food crops and pastures, to be ingested by animals and to get into milk and into babies and children and adolescents whose growing bones were hungry for calcium or its equivalent strontium, in this case radioactive. Incidentally, radiostrontium was known to the biologists before it "hit the headlines." They had found it in the skin burns of animals exposed on the Nevada testing ranges and they knew its sinister nature as a "bone-seeker." But the authorities clapped security on their work, classified it as

"Operation Sunshine" and cynically called the units of radiostrontium "Sunshine Units"—an instance not of ignorance but of deliberate noncommunication.

One beneficial effect of the alarm caused by all this has been that the atoms industry is, bar none, the safest in the world for those working in it. Precautions, now universal, were built into the code of practice from the beginning. Indeed it can be admitted that the safety margins in health and in working conditions are perhaps excessive in the light of experience, but no one would dare to modify them. There can, however, be accidents in which the public assumes the risk. At Windscale, the British atomic center in Cumberland, a reactor burned out. Radioactive fumes escaped from the stacks in spite of the filters. They drifted over the country. Milk was dumped into the sea because radioactive iodine had covered the dairy pastures.

There is the problem of atomic waste disposal, which persists in the peaceful uses as well as in the making of nuclear explosives. Low energy wastes, carefully monitored, can be safely disposed of. Trash, irradiated metals and laboratory waste can be embedded in concrete and dumped in the ocean deeps—although this practice raises some misgivings. But high-level wastes, some with elements the radioactivity of which can persist for hundreds of thousands of years, present prodigious difficulties. There must be "burial grounds" (or, euphemistically, "farms"), the biggest of which is at Hanford, Wash. The Hanford "farm" encloses a stretch of the Columbia River in a tract covering 575 square miles where no one is allowed to live or to trespass.

There, in the 20th-century Giza, it has cost more, much more, to bury live atoms than it cost to entomb the sun-god kings of Egypt. . . .

The alarming possibilities were well illustrated by the incident at Palomares on the coast of Spain, when there occurred a collision of a refueling aircraft with a U.S. nuclear bomber on "live" mission. The bombs were scattered. There was no explosion, but radioactive materials broke loose and the contaminated beaches and farm soil had to be scooped up and taken to the United States for burial.

Imagine what would have happened if the *Torrey Canyon,* the giant tanker which was wrecked off the Scilly Isles, had been nuclear-powered. Some experts make comforting noises and say that the reactors would have "closed down," but the *Torrey Canyon* was a wreck and the Palomares incident showed what happens when radioactive materials break loose. All those oil-polluted beaches of southwest England and the coasts of Brittany would have had to be scooped up for nuclear burial.

The *Torrey Canyon* is a nightmarish example of progress for its own sake. The bigger the tanker, the cheaper the freightage, which is supposed to be progress. This ship was built at Newport News, Va. in 1959 for the Union Oil Company; it was a giant for the time—810 feet long and 104 feet beam—but, five years later, that was not big enough. She was taken to Japan to be "stretched." The ship was cut in half amidship and a mid-body section inserted. With a new bow, this made her 974 feet long, and her beam was extended 21 feet. She could carry 850,000 barrels of oil, twice her original capacity.

Built for Union Oil, she was "owned" by the Barracuda Tanker Corporation, the head office of which is a filing cabinet in Hamilton, Bermuda. She was registered under the Liberian flag of convenience and her captain and crew were Italians recruited in Genoa. Just to complicate the international tangle, she was under charter to the British Petroleum Tanker Company to bring 118,000 tons of crude oil from Kuwait to Milford Haven in Wales, via the Cape of Good Hope. Approaching Lands End, the Italian captain was informed that if he did not reach Milford Haven by 11 p.m. Saturday night he would miss high water and would not be able to enter the harbor for another five days, which would have annoyed his employers. He took a shortcut, setting course between Seven Stones rocks and the Scilly Isles, and he finished up on Pollard Rock, in an area where no ship of that size should ever have been.

Her ruptured tanks began to vomit oil and great slicks appeared over the sea in the direction of the Cornish holiday beaches. A Dutch tug made a dash for the stranded ship, gambling on the salvage money. (Where the salvaged ship could have been taken one cannot imagine, since no place would offer harborage to a leaking tanker.) After delays and a death in the futile salvage effort, the British Government moved in with the navy, the air force and, on the beaches, the army. They tried to set fire to the floating oil which, of course, would not volatilize. They covered the slicks with detergents (supplied at a price by the oil companies), and then the bombers moved in to try to cut open the deck and, with incendiaries, to set fire to the remaining oil in the tanks. Finally the ship foundered and divers confirmed that the oil had been effectively consumed.

Nevertheless the result was havoc. All measures had had to be improvised. Twelve thousand tons of detergent went into the sea. Later marine biologists found that the cure had been worse than the complaint. The oil was disastrous for seabirds, but marine organic life was destroyed by the detergents. By arduous physical efforts, with bulldozers and flamethrowers and, again, more detergents, the beaches were cleaned up for the holiday-makers. Northerly winds swept the oil slicks down Channel to the French coast with even more serious consequences, particularly to the valuable shellfish industry. With even bigger tankers being launched, this affair is a portentous warning.

Two years after *Torrey Canyon,* an offshore oil rig erupted in the Santa Barbara Channel. The disaster to wildlife in this area, which has island nature reserves and is on the migratory route of whales, seals and seabirds, was a repetition of the *Torrey Canyon* oil spill. And the operator of the lethal oil rig was Union Oil.

Another piece of stupidity shows how much we are at the mercy of ignorant men pretending to be knowledgeable. During the International Geophysical Year, 1957-58, the Van Allen Belt was discovered. This is an area of magnetic phenomena. Immediately it was decided to explode a nuclear bomb in the belt to see whether an artificial aurora could be produced. The colorful draperies and luminous skirts of the aurora borealis are caused by the drawing in of cosmic particles through the rare gases of the upper atmosphere—ionization it is called; it is like passing electrons through the vacuum tubes of our familiar fluorescent lighting.

The name Rainbow Bomb was given it in anticipation of the display it was expected to produce. Every eminent scientist in the field of cosmology, radio astronomy or physics of the atmosphere protested at this irresponsible tampering with a system which we did not understand. And, typical of the casual attitude toward this kind of thing, the Prime Minister of the day, answering protests in the House of Commons that called on him to intervene with the Americans, asked what all the fuss was about. After all, they hadn't known that the Van Allen Belt even existed a year before. This was the cosmic equivalent of Chamberlain's remark about Czechoslovakia, at the time of Munich, about that distant country of which we knew so little. They exploded the bomb. They got their pyrotechnics and we still do not know the cost we may have to pay for this artificial magnetic disturbance.

In the same way we can look with misgivings on those tracks—the white tails of the jets that are introducing into our climatic system new factors, the effects of which are immensurable. Formation of rain clouds depends upon water vapor having a nucleus on which to form. That is how artificial precipitation is introduced—the so-called rain-making. So the jets, crisscrossing the weather system, playing noughts and crosses with it, can produce a man-made change.

In the longer term we can foresee even more drastic effects from Man's unthinking operations. At the United Nations' Science and Technology Conference in Geneva in 1963 we took stock of the effects of industrialization on our total environment thus far. The atmosphere is not only the air which humans, animals and plants breathe, it is also the envelope that protects living things from harmful radiation from the sun and outer space. It is also the medium of climate, the winds and the rain. Those are inseparable from the hydrosphere—the oceans, covering seven tenths of the globe, with their currents and extraordinary rates of evaporation; the biosphere, with its trees and their transpiration; and, in terms of human activities, the minerals mined from the lithosphere, the rock crust. Millions of years ago the sun encouraged the growth of the primeval forests, which became our coal, and the plant growth of the seas, which became our oil. Those fossil fuels, locked away for eons of time, are extracted by man and put back into the atmosphere from the chimney stacks and the exhaust pipes of modern engineering. About six billion tons of carbon are mixed with the atmosphere annually. During the past century, in the process of industrialization, with its release of carbon by the burning of fossil fuels, more than 400 billion tons of carbon have been artificially introduced into the atmosphere. The concentration in the air we breathe has been increased by approximately 10%, and if all the known reserves of coal and oil were burned at once the concentration would be 10 times greater.

This is something more than a public health problem, more than a question of what goes into the lungs of an individual, more than a question of smog. The carbon cycle in nature is a self-adjusting mechanism. Carbon dioxide is, of course, indispensable for plants and is, therefore, a source of life, but there is a balance which is maintained by excess carbon being absorbed by the seas. The excess is now taxing this absorption, and it can seriously disturb the heat balance of the earth because of what is known as the "greenhouse effect." A greenhouse lets in the sun's rays but retains the heat. Carbon dioxide, as a transparent diffusion, does likewise. It keeps the heat at the surface of the earth and in excess modifies the climate.

It has been estimated that, at the present rate of increase, the mean annual temperature all over the world might increase by $3.6°$ centigrade in the next 40 to 50 years. The experts may argue about the time factor and even about the effects, but certain things are apparent, not only in the industrialized northern hemisphere but in the southern hemisphere also. The north-polar ice cap is thinning and shrinking. The seas, with their blanket of carbon dioxide, are changing their temperature, with the result that marine plant life is increasing and is transpiring more carbon dioxide. As a result of the combination, fish are migrating, changing even their latitudes. On land the snow line is retreating and glaciers are melting. In Scandinavia, land which was perennially under snow and ice is thawing, and arrowheads of more than 1,000 years ago, when the black soils were last exposed, have been found. The melting of sea ice will not affect the sea level, because the volume of floating ice is the same as the water it displaces, but the melting of ice caps or glaciers, in which the water is locked up, will introduce additional water to the sea and raise the level. Rivers originating in glaciers and permanent snow fields will increase their flow; and if ice dams, such as those in the Himalayas, break, the results in flooding may be catastrophic. In this process the patterns of rainfall will change, with increased precipitation in some areas and the possibility of aridity in now fertile regions. One would be well advised not to take 99-year leases on properties at present sea level.

At that same conference, there was a sobering reminder of mistakes which can be writ large, from the very best intentions. In the Indus Valley in West Pakistan, the population is increasing at the rate of 10 more mouths to be fed every five minutes. In that same five minutes in that same place, an acre of land is being lost through waterlogging and salinity. This is the largest irrigated region in the world. Twenty-three million acres are artificially watered by canals. The Indus and its tributaries, the Jhelum, the Chenab, the Ravi, the Beas and the Sutlej, created the alluvial plains of the Punjab and the Sind. In the 19th century, the British began a big program of farm development in lands which were fertile but had low rainfall. Barrages and distribution canals were constructed. One thing which, for economy's sake, was not done was to line the canals. In the early days, this genuinely did not matter. The water was being spread from the Indus into a thirsty plain and if it soaked in so much the better. The system also depended on what is called "inland delta drainage," that is to say, the water spreads out like a delta and then drains itself back into the river. After independence, Pakistan, with external aid, started vigorously to extend the Indus irrigation. The experts all said the soil was good and would produce abundantly once it got the distributed water. There were plenty of experts, but they all overlooked one thing—the hydrological imperatives. The incline from Lahore to the Rann of Kutch—700 miles—is a foot a mile, a quite inadequate drainage gradient. So as more and more barrages and more and more lateral canals were built, the water was not draining back into the Indus. Some 40% of the water in the unlined canals seeped underground, and in a network of

40,000 miles of canals that is a lot of water. The result was that the water table rose. Low-lying areas became waterlogged, drowning the roots of the crops. In other areas the water crept upward, leaching salts that accumulated in the surface layers, poisoning the crops. At the same time the irrigation regime, which used just 1½ inches of water a year in the fields, did not sluice out those salts but added, through evaporation, its own salts. The result was tragically spectacular. In flying over large tracts of this area, one would imagine that it was an Arctic landscape because the white crust of salt glistens like snow.

The situation was deteriorating so rapidly that President Ayub appealed in person to President Kennedy, who sent out a high-powered mission which encompassed 20 disciplines. This was backed by the computers at Harvard. The answers were pretty grim. It would take 20 years and $2 billion to repair the damage—more than it cost to create the installations that did the damage. It would mean using vertical drainage to bring up the water and use it for irrigation, and also to sluice out the salt in the surface soil. If those 20 scientific disciplines had been brought together in the first instance, it would not have happened.

One more instance of the far-flung consequences of Man's localized mistakes: no insecticides or pesticides have ever been allowed into the continent of Antarctica. Yet they have been found in the fauna along the northern coasts. They have come almost certainly from the northern hemisphere, carried from the rivers of the farm states into the currents sweeping south. In November 1969, the U.S. Government decided to "phase out" the use of DDT.

Pollution is a crime compounded of ignorance and avarice. The great achievements of *Homo sapiens* become the disaster-ridden blunders of unthinking Man— poisoned rivers and dead lakes, polluted with the effluents of industries which give something called "prosperity" at the expense of posterity. Rivers are treated like sewers and lakes like cesspools. These natural systems—and they are living systems—have struggled hard. The benevolent micro-organisms which cope with reasonable amounts of organic matter have been destroyed by mineral detergents. Witness our foaming streams. Lake Erie did its best to provide the oxygen to neutralize the pickling acids of the great steelworks. But it could not contend. It lost its oxygen in the battle. Its once rich commercial fishing industry died and its revitalizing micro-organic life gave place to anaerobic organisms which do not need oxygen but give off foul smells, the mortuary smells of dead water. As one Erie industrialist retorted, "It's not our effluent; it's those damned dead fish."

We have had the Freedom from Hunger Campaign; presently we shall need a Freedom from Thirst Campaign. If the International Hydrological Decade does not bring us to our senses, we will face a desperate situation. Of course it is bound up with the increasing population, but also with the extravagances of the technologies which claim that they are serving that population. There is a competition between the water needs of the land which has to feed the increasing population and the domestic and industrial needs of that population. The theoretical minimum to sustain living standards is about 300 gallons a day per person. This is the approximate amount of water needed to produce grain for 2½ pounds of bread, but a diet of two pounds of bread and one pound of beef would require about 2,500 gallons. And that is nothing compared with the gluttonous requirements of steel-making, paper-making and the chemical industry.

Water—just H_2O—is as indispensable as food. To die of hunger one needs more than 15 days. To die of thirst one needs only three. Yet we are squandering, polluting and destroying water. In Los Angeles and neighboring Southern California, a thousand times more water is being consumed than is being precipitated in the locality. They have preempted the water of neighboring states. They are piping it from Northern California, and there is a plan to pipe it all the way from Canada's Northwest Territories, from the Mackenzie and the Liard, which flow northward to the Arctic Ocean, to turn them back into deserts.

Always and everywhere we come back to the problem of population—more people to make more mistakes, more people to be the victims of the mistakes of others, more people to suffer hell upon earth. It is appalling to hear people complacently talking about the population explosion as though it belonged to the future, or world hunger as though it were threatening, when hundreds of millions can testify that it is already here—swear it with panting breath.

We know to the exact countdown second when the nuclear explosion took place—5:30 a.m., July 16, 1945, when the first device went off in the desert of Alamogordo, N. Mex. The fuse of the population explosion had been lit 10 years earlier—February 1935. On that day a girl called Hildegarde was dying of generalized septicemia. She had pricked her finger with a sewing needle and the infection had run amok. The doctors could not save her. Her desperate father injected a red dye into her body. Her father was Gerhard Domagk. The red dye was prontosil, which he, a pharmaceutical chemist, had produced and had successfully used on mice lethally infected with streptococci, but never before on a human. Prontosil was the first of the sulfa drugs—chemotherapeutics—which could attack the germ within the living body. Thus was prepared the way for the rediscovery of penicillin —rediscovery because, although Fleming had discovered it in 1928, it had been ignored; neither he nor anybody else had seen its supreme virtue of attacking germs within the living body. That is the operative phrase, for while medical science and the medical profession had used antiseptics for surface wounds and sores, they were always labeled "Poison, not to be taken internally." The sulfa drugs had shown that it was possible to attack specific germs within the living body and had changed this attitude. So when Chain and Florey looked again at Fleming's penicillin in 1938, they were seeing it in the light of the experience of the sulfas.

A new era of disease-fighting had begun—the sulfas, the antibiotics, DDT insecticides. Doctors could now attack a whole range of invisible enemies. They could master the old killer diseases. They proved it during the war, and when the war ended there were not only stockpiles of the drugs, there were tooled-up factories to produce them. So, to prevent the spread of the deadly epidemics which follow wars, the supplies were made available to the war-ravaged countries with their displaced persons, and then to the developing countries. Their indigenous infections and contagions and insect-borne diseases were checked.

Almost symbolically, the first great clinical use of prontosil had been in dealing with puerperal sepsis, childbed fever. It had spectacularly saved mothers' lives in Queen Charlotte's Hospital, London. Now its successors took up the story. Fewer mothers died in childbirth, to live and have more babies. Fewer infants died, fewer toddlers, fewer adolescents. They lived to marry and have children. Older people were not killed off by, for instance, malaria. The average life-span increased.

Professor Kingsley Davis of the University of California at Berkeley, the authority on urban development, has presented a hair-raising picture from his survey of the world's cities. He has shown that 38% of the world's population is already living in what are defined as urban places. More than one fifth of the world's population is living in cities of 100,000 or more. And more than one tenth of the world's population is now living in cities of a million or more inhabitants. In 1968, 375 million people were living in million-and-over cities. The proportions are changing so quickly that on present trends it would take only 16 years for half the world's population to be living in cities and only 55 years for it to reach 100%.

Within the lifetime of a child born today, Kingsley Davis foresees, on present trends of population increase, 15 billion people to be fed and housed—nearly five times as many as now. The whole human species would be living in cities of a million and over inhabitants, and—wait for it!—the biggest city would have 1.3 billion inhabitants. That means 186 times as many as there are in Greater London.

For years the Greek architect Doxiadis has been warning us about such prospects. In his Ecumenopolis—World City—one urban area would ooze into the next, like confluent ulcers. The East Side of World City would have as its High Street the Eurasian Highway stretching from Glasgow to Bangkok, with the Channel Tunnel as its subway and a built-up area all the way. On the West Side of World City, divided not by the tracks but by the Atlantic, the pattern is already emerging, or rather, merging. Americans already talk about Boswash, the urban development of a built-up area stretching from Boston to Washington; and on the West Coast, apart from Los Angeles sprawling into the desert, the realtors are already slurring one city into another all along the Pacific Coast from the Mexican border to San Francisco. We don't need a crystal ball to foresee what Davis and Doxiadis are predicting; we can already see it through smog-covered spectacles. A blind man can smell what is coming.

The danger of prediction is that experts and men of affairs are likely to plan for the predicted trends and confirm these trends. "Prognosis" is something different from "Prediction." An intelligent doctor, having diagnosed your symptoms and examined your condition, does not say (except in novelettes), "You have six months to live." An intelligent doctor says, "Frankly, your condition is serious. Unless you do so-and-so, and I do so-and-so, it is bound to deteriorate." The operative phrase is "do so-and-so." We don't have to plan for trends; if they are socially undesirable our duty is to plan away from them, to treat the symptoms before they become malignant.

We have to do this on the local, the national and the international scale, through intergovernmental action, because there are no frontiers in present-day pollution and destruction of the biosphere. Mankind shares a common habitat. We have mortgaged the old homestead and nature is liable to foreclose.

3

Nature Abused

The Earth is characterized by change. Natural occurrences alter the ecology of regions constantly, some temporarily, some permanently. But no force has effected such precipitous and radical changes upon the Earth as has humanity. Human beings, by their interference in the life cycles of this planet, can move the evolutionary processes of nature at phenomenal speeds, even initiate irreversible changes. Abuse of nature has been a recurrent theme in history as people have indelibly scarred the Earth and its creatures.

Through attempts to create an environment that is more comfortable, more compatible with their desires, more abundant with the necessities of human life, people have killed off entire species, eliminated forests, exhausted the land through injudicious agricultural methods, gobbled up the Earth's store of fuel, destroyed rivers and lakes by making them garbage dumps. As Clarence Glacken shows in the first selection that follows, even in the reputedly rational era of classical Greece people assumed the role of master and controller of nature. Glacken draws upon literary evidence to demonstrate that the ancients combined a passionate reverence for nature with an equally zealous expectation that they should control and shape the environment in their own interests. The Greeks and Romans, in spite of their profound feeling for nature, assumed that they should have full power to control, direct, and shape nature, and they engaged in intensive exploitation of the soil and the forests. The long-term result was erosion or exhaustion of vast tracts of land and the ultimate ruination of once fertile and productive areas.

The overuse of agricultural land is discernible all over the globe. Despite differences in attitudes between the Greeks of the fifth century B.C., described by

Glacken, and the midwestern American farmers of the 1930s, the tragic results have been the same: erosion and waste of soil resources. Earley Wilcox provides yet another example. He examined soil erosion in China before the Communist Revolution of 1949. He reports that the Yangtse and Yellow, as well as the Ganges and other major rivers of Asia, run thick with silt washed from the loose soil at the headwater regions that have been grossly overused as agricultural bases for millions of people for generations. Clearly, erosion resulting from misuse of the land is not a new problem, nor a uniquely Western one.

The abuse of nature's waterways has economic and aesthetic consequences as well as a serious ecological impact. For example, in the late Middle Ages the port city of Bruges at the mouth of the Rhine River lost its prominence as a commercial center after heavy silting closed its harbor and river access routes. And the problem of silting and pollution of rivers and lakes plagues modern society on a scale never before experienced. Perhaps the case of Lake Erie, twelfth largest lake in the world and now threatened with biological death, makes this point too painfully clear. Kenneth Slocum gives an idea of the effect the stepped-up pollution of the industrial era has had on nature. He reports that the oil-slicked Cuyahoga River and dozens of similar tributaries that feed into Lake Erie have filled it with such a collection of human waste and factory sludge that it has been aged artificially by 15,000 years in only the fifty years that it has served as a cesspool for this industrial society.

Humanity's mutilating effect upon the Earth is quite visable in the long history of depletion of other natural resources as well. For thousands of years we have menaced Earth's forests; we have slashed and cut away about one half of the globe's original woodland covering. From ancient to modern times people have ruthlessly cleared trees from the land to make room for cultivation, for cities, freeways, and a thousand other human enterprises. The famous stands of cedars of Lebanon have been turned into a desert; in England deforestation had already reached alarming proportions by the age of Elizabeth I; and today in the United States the forests are challenged on an unprecedented scale—not even the tiny groves of majestic redwoods, which have stood as a symbol of natural beauty and strength since before the birth of Christ, are secure from human rapaciousness. Marc Bloch has studied deforestation in medieval France, and he demonstrates that the relentless assault upon the wilderness had a devastating impact upon the woodlands and upon the nature of early medieval society itself. A change in the ecological balance, such as the one Bloch discusses, forces social adjustment in the wake of environmental transformations.

Forests have been assaulted for fuel, for lumber products, and to make way for agriculture and "progress" in general. As the woodlands began to disappear and as human beings required the environment to furnish more and more fuel, they turned to fossil fuels: coal, oil, and gas from below the ground. It took hundreds of millions of years for these massive yet finite fuel deposits to accumulate, yet in the past century they have been depleted with such amazing efficiency that they are already running short, another victim of industrialism and wanton exploitation.

Among the most brutal chapters in the story of humanity's tenency on Earth has been the abuse of other animals. Since prehistoric times people have destroyed countless numbers of other creatures—even making many varieties extinct by narrowing their natural range through changes in the habitat and by simple overkill. Paul Martin hypothesizes that *Homo sapiens,* the compulsive hunter, totally extinguished a fantastic number of large land animals in North America and Africa long before civilization. Our prehistoric ancestors engaged in an overkill policy that annihilated such large mammals as the woolly mammoth, the saber-toothed tiger, and many others. Of course, these prehistoric peoples were less efficient than their modern counterparts who have engineered the obliteration of vast numbers of creatures *and* their habitat in a very short period. Prehistoric hunters required many centuries to work their way through primal herds; modern hunters need no more than a few decades. Less than a century ago the passenger pigeon was so numerous that passing flocks blocked out the sun for hours and broke the branches of trees when they went to roost. Uncontrollable human violence wiped out these birds in a few years, sending them the way of the dodo, another victim and the very symbol of extinction. The only remaining passenger pigeons are stuffed museum exhibits, the mute yet eloquent remains of an entire species and of a time now lost forever.

There is perhaps no better example of the wanton attack upon wildlife than the destruction of the buffalo. They teemed in herds of millions over the grasslands of North America in the nineteenth century. In less than a century the advancing frontier of civilization swept over them; they were slaughtered indiscriminately and brought to the very threshold of extinction; and the aboriginal peoples who depended upon the buffalo for their own survival were correspondingly threatened.

Although the slaughter of the buffalo stopped just in time to save it from extinction, modern peoples have not altered their basic relationship with lesser animals. Destruction and extinction still move in the shadow of human progress. As they reach astounding numbers and as they attain the technological means of mass destruction, human beings become an even more devastating threat to wildlife. Rachel Carson demonstrates with powerful feeling that people today, through the use of deadly pesticides and agricultural chemicals, have launched a policy of overkill that not only threatens lesser species in an unprecedented manner but endangers humanity as well through pesticide pollution.

One cannot help but notice the recurrence of a theme stressed by Glacken in regard to the Greeks: human beings attempt to bring order to the world and to control their environment. But they have been frustrated in this endeavor; they never truly control the environment, they only do battle with it and inflict terrible wounds upon it. Their efforts to alter their surroundings to suit their purposes have brought disaster; the specter of tragedy stalks humanity's accomplishment on Earth.

Clarence J. Glacken

Changing Ideas
of the Habitable World

The reason that Attica in former times could support a soldiery exempt from the toil of farming, says Plato in his *Critias,* was that its soil—as is proved by the remnant now left—surpassed all others in fertility. Deluges, however, washed the soil down from the mountains, and it was lost because the land dropped abruptly into the sea. Attica became a "skelton of a body wasted by disease." Long ago, Plato continues, there were abundant forests in the mountains which provided fodder for the animals and storage for water, which could then issue forth in springs and rivers. "The water was not lost, as it is today, by running off a barren ground to the sea." The extent of these forests, many of which had been cut down, was revealed in the traces still remaining and by the sanctuaries which were situated at the former sources of springs and rivers. . . .

Plato reconstructs the prehistory of Attica by showing how the relict soils reveal ancient conditions of the plains and how the relict trees reveal the ancient conditions of the mountains, suggesting that human history was in part the history of environmental changes induced by natural catastrophes and human activities. Perhaps if this view had found more elaborate expression in the *Laws,* in which Plato discusses the origin and development of society, an awareness of the philosophical implications of man's activities in changing the environment might have at that time entered the main stream of Western thought. . . .

Across the Eurasian continent, Mencius, the Chinese philosopher, described the beautiful trees of the new mountain which were hewn down with axes. When they began growing again, buds and sprouts appeared, and cattle and goats browsed upon them. "To these things is owing the bare and stripped appearance of the mountain, and when people now see it, they think it was never finely wooded. But is this the nature of the mountain?" Few statements have summed up more lucidly than has this question of Mencius the difficulties of distinguishing a natural from a cultural landscape. . . .

In the third century B.C. Eratosthenes described the manner in which the island of Cyprus was made habitable. Formerly its plains could not be used for agriculture because they were covered with forests. Felling trees in order to provide fuel for smelting copper and silver mined there helped to clear the forests, and, "as the sea was now navigated with security and by a large naval force," additional clearings were made for ship timber. These cuttings were not sufficient to clear the forests, and the people therefore were allowed to cut down the trees "to hold the land thus cleared as their own property, free from all payments". . . . Eratosthenes thus relates the changes in the landscape to mining, navigation, and governmental land policy.

Early observations such as these failed to inspire men to study the environmental changes made by human cultures as a part of human history. The reason for this failure is not that human modifications of the environment were so inconsequential as to be unworthy of remark but that the emphasis was on human society, its origin, and the manner of its changing through historical time.

THE GOLDEN AGE AND THE IDEA OF CYCLES

In the Greek notion of a past golden age with its "golden race of mortal men," nature which had not felt the intrusions of human art was considered more perfect and fruitful. "The bounteous earth," Hesiod said, "bare first for them of her own will, in plenty and without stint." Similar statements were made centuries later by Lucretius, Varro, and Ovid. . . . The praise of the fertile soils of the golden age, which did not require cultivation, was probably a reflection of contemporary dissatisfaction with the modest yields obtained by hard work.

The idea of a cycle in the course of history, or in the growth of states and institutions—an analogy derived from the life-cycle of an organism—was in antiquity an alternative conception to the notion of degeneration from a golden age. Epicurus and Lucretius applied the cyclical theory to the earth itself, which in its prime spontaneously yielded crops, vines, fruits, and pastures that now even with toil could not be made to grow. A son should not complain about his father's good luck or rail at heaven because of his old and wilted vines: "nor does he grasp that all things waste away little by little and pass to the grave fordone by age and the lapse of life." . . .

Later in the poem, however, Lucretius, following Epicurus, traces the origin of metallurgy to the accidental smelting of ores heated by forest fires which may have been started by lightning, or by men who wished to frighten enemies concealed in the woods, to enlarge their fields or pastures, or to kill the wild animals for profit, for hunting by the use of pitfalls and fire was an earlier development than driving game with dogs into fenced-in glades. . . .

The landscapes of inhabited lands were created by imitating nature; man had learned how to domesticate nature by sowing, grafting, and experimenting with plants. "And day by day they would constrain the woods more and more to retire up the mountains, and to give up the land beneath to tilth" to have meadows, pools, streams, crops, vineyards, and olive orchards. . . . Lucretius clearly is describing here, in poetical language and without any suggestion of decay and death, the manner in which a people transforms the landscape.

ANOTHER NATURE

The early history of the idea of man as a modifier of his environment is also related to the broader conception, similar to the cyclical theory, of a teleology existent in a single organism or in all nature—a conception fully developed by Aristotle in his discussion of the four causes. The fruit of the tree was inherent in the seed; so was a design implicit in the living creation. Since man was the highest creature, all nature must have been created for him, an idea which must be one of the oldest of which there is a written record, for it is clearly expressed in ancient Egyptian creation myths.

In the idea of a design in nature, as it was developed by the Greeks and their Roman disciples, a pleasant and harmonious relation between man and nature is either expressed or implied, for human art improves the natural advantages of an earth which has been created as a home for man. This idea is discussed by Aristotle, . . . Cicero, Seneca, . . . and Pliny, . . . Cicero's exposition being the most detailed. The earth endowed with living nature, said Cicero, is the proper home both for the gods and for man, man taking an active part in the care of nature by cultivating the earth so that its fertility would not be choked with weeds. There is an order of nature existing on earth—which is eternal—an order in which the great variety of organic species is arranged in an ascending scale. Man, as the highest being in the scale, changes nature by using his hands, with which, guided by the intellect, he has created the art of agriculture and the techniques of fishing, animal domestication, mining, clearing, and navigation. . . .

> We are the absolute masters of what the earth produces. We enjoy the mountains and the plains. The rivers are ours. We sow the seed, and plant the trees. We fertilize the earth. . . . We stop, direct, and turn the rivers: in short by our hands we endeavor, by our various operations in this world, to make, as it were, another Nature. . . .

The concept of "another," the man-made nature, thus seems a fusion of two elements: the design inherent in nature and the improvements of nature which are interpreted as the effects brought about by human art in fulfillment of the design.

SOIL AND AGRICULTURE

In the technical agricultural writings of antiquity, comments regarding human changes of nature also appear in discussions of land use and of soil fertility. These writings, from Hesiod through Vergil and Pliny, are concerned for the most part with technical details, the Roman writers particularly emphasizing farm management and the cultivation of the olive and the vine. One significant fact about them is the association of soil conservation with agriculture—an association which has persisted in modern, even contemporary, times in discussions regarding population and food supply, in which the chief emphasis has been on the care and fertilization of arable land.

Perhaps the earliest idea is that the soils must be allowed to rest, because cultivation tires them. "Fallow-land," said Hesiod, "is a guardian-from-death-and-ruin, and a soother of children. . . . There is a similar idea in the Old Testament, . . . the Lord commanding that every seventh year be a "sabbath of rest unto the land."

Two Roman writers, Varro and Columella, are significant in this history, because their writings, revealing the influence of Stoic philosophy, dealt with questions which transcended the technical details of agriculture.

Varro said that human life had developed from the original state of nature "when man lived on those things which the virgin earth produced spontaneously"—another reminder of the strength of the idea that soil fertility was characteristic of a golden age. From the state of nature mankind passed through a pastoral stage of gathering and animal domestication followed by the agricultural stage that lasted until the rise of contemporary civilization. . . .

This theory and its modern successors diverted attention from the actual historical events, since cultural development presumably took place regardless of the nature of the physical environment. The first serious challenge to this sequence was delayed, as Carl Sauer . . . has said, until Alexander von Humboldt attacked the theory, because pastoral nomadism was not found in the New World. Since Varro's time, however, abstract theories of cultural development have evaded the question of how man was changing his environment as he marched through these stages.

Varro was far more sensible than his latter-day imitators, for he saw an exception to his theory in his own time and in his own country: heads of families have deserted the land for the cities and have imported corn and wine from foreign countries. "And so in that country where the city's founders were shepherds and taught agriculture to their descendants, these descendants have reversed the process, and through covetousness and in despite of laws, have turned corn-land into meadow, not knowing the difference between agriculture and grazing." . . . Agriculture was creative; grazing, extractive. "Grazing cattle do not help to produce what grows on the land; they remove it with their teeth." . . .

In his work on agriculture Columella comments approvingly on the opinions of a certain Tremelius that the productivity of land declines rapidly after a clearing; plows break the roots of the plants, and the trees no longer provide organic materials for fertilizer—a sentence reminding one of current discussions of the exhaustion of tropical soils a few years after they have been cleared and cultivated. . . . Columella is significant as a thinker, however, because he objected to the analogy of the earth as a mortal being; his work begins with an attack, probably aimed at the Epicureans and Lucretius, on the popular view that the earth had a life-cycle: "It is not, therefore, because of weariness, as very many have believed, nor because of old age, but manifestly because of our own lack of energy that our cultivated lands yield us a less generous return. For we may reap greater harvests if the earth is quickened again by frequent, timely, and moderate manuring." . . . Instead of a philosophy of the earth as a mortal being, the practical Columella substitutes manuring.

The *Natural History* of Pliny gives further evidence of a lively awareness in antiquity of the effects of human activities on the earth. Pliny says, too, that a soil should not be regarded as old in a mortal sense. Soils would last with care, and in cultivating hillsides it was not necessary to denude them if the digging were done skillfully. He also describes how the emptying of a lake in the Larissa district of Thessaly lowered the temperature of the vicinity, causing the olive to disappear and the vines to be frostbitten, how the climate of Aenos on the Maritza became warmer when the river was diverted near it, and how Philippi altered its climate when its land under cultivation was drained. . . .

INFLUENCE OF THE PHYSICAL ENVIRONMENT

Another influential body of thought, the theory of the influence of the physical environment on human cultures, owes its origin to the thinkers of antiquity. This literature, both in antiquity and in modern times, has dealt with the influence of climate, soils, and geographical location on individuals and on cultures. Its main outlines may be traced through the Hippocratic writings, Herodotus, Thucydides, Aristotle, Polybius, Pliny, and Vitruvius, although the ancient writers on the whole were far less rigid in their determinism than many thinkers of the eighteenth and nineteenth centuries.

The significance of these theories is that they led to a one-sided preoccupation with environmental influences, largely ignoring the significance of man as an agent in changing the environment; in ancient and modern times both ideas were often expressed by the same writer without any realization of an implied contradiction.

Earley Vernon Wilcox

Acres and People

The problem of loss and devastation of soil by erosion arose in both India and China in the same manner and from similar causes. The mountain hillbilly tribes of India especially in Bhutan and Nepal in the foothills of the Himalayas have been left largely to their own devices. The British have hestitated to interfere with them. As their numbers increase they clear more forest land by the ax and fire, using the new land for crops or pasture. They are rather footloose nomads and abandon these

From *Acres and People: The Eternal Problem of China and India* by Earley Vernon Wilcox, pp. 132-139. Published by Orange Judd Publishing Company, Inc., 1947.

clearings within a few years for other locations. Consequently under the annual monsoon rainfall of 250 inches in these high Himalayan catchment basins great gullies are formed by the dashing mountain streams, the underlying rocks are denuded of their soil covering, and this soil in constantly increasing quantities is carried down into Bengal. In 1650 Bengal Province was described by eye witnesses as more abundantly fertile than the Nile Valley. Calcutta once abutted on a bay but it is now miles up from the mouth of the Ganges which flows through a channel between mud banks of silt from eroded mountain land. And today there is general agreement that the soils of Bengal are deficient in plant food materials as a result of leaching by the monsoon floods and from their lack of nitrogen due to the scanty use of animal manure. "The soil reached its state of maximum impoverishment many years ago."

In China the great drainage systems of the Hwang Ho and Yangtse Rivers rise in the Kuenlun Mountains of Tibet. China never had complete control of that region. Heavy spring rains and melting snows of hundreds of feet depth provide flood water that rushes down the mountain slopes carrying silt, sand and gravel to the valleys below. Even boulders up to a foot in diameter are rolled along in the stream beds. The pastoral tribes in the upper reaches of these rivers are notoriously indifferent to soil preservation. Forests are felled, land cleared by fire, and when the grass cover appears, it in turn is destroyed by overgrazing. Such tribes of nomads have created dire trouble for farmers not only in China and India but also in Persia, Iraq, the Near East, and elsewhere. In fact, the world over, river-borne silt automatically limits the useful life of irrigation dams. No matter how high these dams may be, sooner or later they are doomed to become completely filled with silt and therefore useless.

The serious problem presented by the Yangtse River is described by Shao Shang Lee:—

In the autumn of 1931 came the great Yangtse River flood, which affected nearly 25 million people. To keep the river from overflowing again strong dikes were built. Under the leadership of Sir John Hope Simpson and some two hundred Chinese engineers, a million Chinese laborers within six months repaired and built 1,473 miles of dikes and completed 73 miles of new channeling work to improve drainage. Many of the dikes were 140 feet broad at the base, 30 feet thick at the top, and 30 to 50 feet high.

Perhaps the most famous case of the silting of river beds by the deposition of soil carried from farther up stream is the Hwang Ho, or Yellow River, known as "China's Sorrow." Dr. W. C. Lowdermilk spent five years or more studying the cantankerous behavior of this river and has presented in various government publications the essential facts of its long recorded history. Even the tourist, who crosses the Yellow Sea in a coasting steamer and notices that for a hundred miles out from shore the water is a sort of tawny consommé, begins to ask questions about the doings of the Yellow River. And should he sojourn in Peking in mid-winter and acquire what feels like a burning nasal catarrh he will be told if he consults a physician that the trouble is due to minute silica crystals carried by the north west winds for hundreds of miles from the great stretches of dry loose soils along the upper Hwang Ho. In fact the atmosphere is distinctly yellow from the fine particles of this soil.

As Dr. Lowdermilk describes his first sight of the Yellow River,

> Here lay the river in a channel 40 to 50 feet above the plain. This gigantic river had been lifted up from the plain over its entire 400-mile course across the delta and had been held in this elevated channel for 600 years by hand labor, without machines, engines or cable. Millions of farmers with bare hands through the centuries had built this monument to the will to survive. For 4000 years the fight had gone on, building dyke after dyke to hold the river in bounds.
>
> All this time as the river heavily laden with brown soil from the highlands reached the sluggish slope of the delta, the silt fell to the bottom and so ceaselessly lifted the river bed. Year after year the farmers must build the dykes higher and higher. In 1852 after being held in the same series of dykes for 600 years the river broke out of its elevated channel and raged across the Province of Honan to the Gulf of Chihli 400 miles north of its former outlet.

If one desires a demonstration of a similar process nearer home he has but to travel along the Mississippi from Memphis to the Gulf of Mexico. The Father of Waters often breaks through the dykes and floods thousand of acres.

Likewise in India, particularly along the Jumna River Valley, floods have gullied large areas of farm lands cutting the country into series of ridges and deep ravines impossible to till. In the Deccan region the fields are so badly scoured by the monsoon rains as to substantially reduce their productivity, the soil loss even on gentle slopes being estimated at 50 to 150 tons per acre annually.

Methods for successfully controlling erosion have been put into practice here and there in India and China. On a large tea plantation near Darjeeling at an elevation of 7,000 feet and with a heavy rainfall the slope of some of the tea gardens is so precipitate that one needs a cane or alpenstock to get about. The land was so terraced and the tea bushes so spaced as to prevent erosion, even where land slides occurred on the steepest declivities and the soil could be held in place only by deeply driven stakes.

On the head waters of the Yellow River Dr. Lowdermilk found that the forests held sacred around temples entirely prevented the erosion which was frightfully destructive on neighboring deforested areas where the soil was gashed by gullies 600 feet deep. A large part of China's forests have been destroyed, the better remaining timbered areas being in Manchuria and Tibet. China's forests are about 45 percent conifers. Only about 7 percent of the land area is in forest as compared with 80 percent in Ceylon.

Before the advent of man trees and herbage anchored the soil with their roots. The deeper the soil the better it suited the grass and forest. The moment soil is uncovered vegetation starts replacing the green carpet. Hardy weeds appear within a few weeks. I have seen lava flows supporting a respectable flora of plants within three years after the molten magma was vomited from the earth. But it can't be done overnight. It's time we ceased blaming nature for soil erosion.

Kenneth G. Slocum

The Dying Lake

CLEVELAND—The oil-slicked Cuyahoga River, which oozes its way through this city to Lake Erie, catches fire periodically, earning it the dubious title of "the only body of water ever classified as a fire hazard."

The bacteria count of the chocolate-brown river water, which bubbles like a witch's brew because of fermenting gases on the bottom, often matches that of pure sewage. The river's mouth, once a wonderful spot to catch black bass, now is so contaminated that surprised scientists have found it doesn't even contain sludge-worms, which thrive on waste. Moreover, most local folks agree, the Cuyahoga stinks.

The Cuyahoga and dozens of other polluted Lake Erie tributaries are the focus of a historic and stormy struggle to save the fourth largest of the Great Lakes from becoming useless to man.

"Lake Erie represents the first large-scale warning that we are in danger of destroying the habitability of the earth," says Barry Commoner, a Washington University biologist and critic of current efforts to curb Erie pollution. "Mankind is in an environmental crisis, and Lake Erie constitutes the biggest warning."

A "BIOLOGICAL EXPLOSION"

Not all pollution experts will go that far, but there is general agreement on one thing: In little more than 50 years, man has wrought on the world's 12th largest lake a startling ecological change. And, biologists agree, the lake may be on the verge of a "biological explosion." They also agree, however, that there's still a lot they don't know about Lake Erie. "We're only now beginning to understand the lake," says one biologist.

Experts figure the 9,940-square-mile lake, gouged by glaciers 12,000 years ago, has been artificially "aged" 15,000 years in the past half century. The obvious by-products of pollution and aging abound. For 40 miles along the Cleveland area, Lake Erie waters, contaminated with slugs of raw sewage, human excrement, oil and chemicals, are generally unfit for swimming.

Algae, organisms invisible to the eye in a healthy lake, litter the Erie shoreline in long rotting piles, clog city water intakes and add objectionable taste to many communities' drinking water. During summer, the algae collect in the western basin in an 800-square-mile mass two feet thick, turning the lake into a solution resembling pea soup.

KILLING FISH AND DUCKS

Pollution also has killed most of the lake's commercial and game fish, such as northern pike, blue pike, sturgeon and cisco. Now the lake is populated by scavenger varieties, such as suckers and carp, which have little commercial value. In addition, the pollution is a significant factor in the sharp decline of wild ducks on Lake Erie and its tributaries. On the Detroit River, where in 1899 ducks were so plentiful one hunting club bagged 122 in a single hour, 10,000 ducks were destroyed by oil pollution in 1960 and huge numbers have shared similar fates each year since then, according to Federal wildlife experts.

Marc Bloch

Medieval Land Clearance

Around the year 1050—in some favored regions such as Normandy and Flanders perhaps a little earlier, in others somewhat later—a new era dawned, which was to last until the late thirteenth century. This was the period of large-scale land clearances, and to all appearance it saw the most considerable additions to the total area of land under cultivation in this country since prehistoric times.

Man's most formidable obstacle was the forests, and it was in the forests that his efforts bore most obvious fruit.

The trees had for centuries halted the progress of the plough. Neolithic farmers, who probably enjoyed a drier climate than our own, set their villages in

From "The Age of Large-Scale Land Clearance" from *French Rural History: An Essay on its Basic Characteristics* by Marc Bloch, translated by Janet Sondheimer. Orginally published by the University of California Press; reprinted by permission of The Regents of the University of California and Rouledge & Kegan Paul Ltd.

expanses of grassland, scrubland, heathland and steppe; the primitive implements at their disposal would have been inadequate for the task of deforestation. In Roman and Frankish times the efforts of woodsmen were apparently more successful. In the early ninth century for example, when Tancred needed land for his completely new village of Le Nocle, he took it from dense forest, *de densitate silvarum.* But even when there were no cultivated clearings, these forests of the early Middle Ages, the ancient forests of France, were by no means unexploited or empty of men.

The forest had its own population, often highly suspect in the eyes of more sedentary folk, who roamed about the woods or lived in shacks they built themselves: huntsmen, charcoal-burners, blacksmiths, gatherers of wax and wild honey (described in the texts as *bigres*), dealers in wood-ash, which was important in the manufacture of glass and soap, and bark-strippers, whose wares were used for tanning hides or could be plaited to make cords. At the end of the twelfth century the lady of Valois employed four servants in her woods at Viry: one was an assarter (this was when land clearance was just beginning), one a trapper, a third an archer and the last an "ash-man." Hunting in the shady forest was not merely a pleasant sport; it also produced hides for urban and seigneurial tanneries and for the binderies of monastic libraries; it supplied meat for everyone, including fighting-men—in 1269 Alphonse de Poitiers ordered the slaughter of a large number of wild boars from his great forests in the Auvergne, to provide salted carcasses for taking overseas on his projected crusade. In an age when the primeval instinct of foraging was nearer the surface than it is today, the forest had greater riches to offer than we perhaps appreciate. People naturally went there for wood, a far greater necessity of life than in this age of oil, petrol and metal; wood was used for heating and lighting (in torches), for building material (roof slats, castle palisades), for footwear (sabots), for plough handles and various other implements, and as faggots for strengthening roadways. There was also a demand for a wide variety of vegetable products, for mosses or dried leaves as bedding, for beechmast on account of the oil, for wild hops and the tart fruit of wild trees—apple, pear, cherry and plum—as also for some of the trees themselves (pear and apple), which were dug up to be used as orchard grafts. But the principal economic contribution of the forest was in a role we no longer demand of it: the presence of fresh leaves, young shoots, grass in the undergrowth, acorns and beechmast made it a first-rate grazing ground. For centuries, in the absence of any standard measurement, the commonest way of indicating the size of a stretch of forest was by reference to the number of pigs it could sustain. Neighboring villagers sent their cattle into the forest, great lords kept vast herds there and even set up stud-farms for their horses. These hordes of animals lived almost in a state of nature, and the habit died hard; even in the sixteenth century, the squire of Gouberville in Normandy had to take to the woods at certain times of the year to round up his stock, and could fail to find them all at one fell swoop. Once he met only the bull "who was limping," "whom no-one had seen for two months past"; on another day his servants managed to catch "the wild mares . . . whom for two years none had contrived to take."

As a result of this relatively intensive and quite unregulated exploitation the ranks of the trees became progressively thinner. Bark-stripping alone must have accounted for many a fine oak. By the eleventh and twelfth centuries, despite the obstructions offered by dead tree-trunks and some remaining thickets where pene-tration was difficult, there were already places where the woodland was sparse. Abbot Suger's foresters were doubtful whether the forest of Iveline could produce the twelve massive timbers he needed for his basilica; Sugar himself regarded the happy discovery which crowned his work as little short of a miracle. The hand of man and the tooth of beast had between them created such havoc among standing timber that the way was prepared for clearance on a larger scale. Even so, the great forests of the early Middle Ages were still so isolated from communal life that they remained largely outside the network of parochial organization which covered every inhabited area.

During the twelfth and thirteenth centuries deliberate efforts were made to bring them in. Patches of tilled land, *ipso facto* liable to tithe, could now be seen at every turn, and their tillers took up permanent residence. Forests on the uplands, hillsides and alluvial lowlands all came under attack from hatchet, billhook and fire. Very few, perhaps none, were totally destroyed, but a large number were reduced to a small remnant of their former extent. They often lost their names as well. There had been a time when, in common with rivers and the principal relief features, each of these sombre smudges on the agrarian landscape had its own place in a geographical vocabulary which descended from a period older than any whose memory has been conserved in the historic languages. By the end of the Middle Ages the ancient entities once known as Bière, Iveline, Laye, Cruye and Loge were reduced to fragments whose names were borrowed from a neighboring hunting-lodge or township, Fontainebleau, Rambouillet, Saint-Germain, Marly and Orleans. Henceforward the forest was to be first and foremost the hunting-ground of kings and nobles. At much the same time as lowlands were losing their covering of trees, peasants of Dauphiné were mounting their attack on alpine forests which had already been broached from within by the settlements of hermit monks.

It would be a mistake, however, to assume that land-clearance was achieved solely by uprooting trees. There was also much activity in marshlands, particularly along the coasts of Flanders and in Bas-Poitou, and on many uncultivated wastes formerly covered with thickets or wild grasses. The chronicle of Morigny . . . tells us that brushwood, brambles, bracken and "all such obstructive plants rooted in the bowels of the earth" were enemies attacked by peasants armed with plough and hoe.

Paul S. Martin

Pleistocene Overkill

About ten thousand years ago, as glaciers retreated into Canada and as man moved southward at the end of the last Ice Age, North America suddenly and strangely lost most of its large animals. Native North American mammals exceeding 100 pounds in adult body weight were reduced by roughly 70 percent. The casualty list includes mammoths, mastodon, many species of horses and camels, four genera of ground sloths, two of peccary, shrub oxen, antelope, two genera of saber-toothed cats, the dire wolf, the giant beaver, tapirs, and others totaling over 100 species. Despite this fantastic loss of large animals during the Pleistocene, the most recent geologic epoch, the fossil record shows no loss of small vertebrates, plants, aquatic organisms, or marine life.

One need not be a Pleistocene geologist to ask the obvious question: What happened? To date there is no obvious answer, certainly not one acceptable to any consensus of scientists interested in the mystery. The question of just what occurred to bring about this unprecedented extinction continues to provoke a storm of controversy.

Extinction, we know, is not an abnormal fate in the life of a species. When all the niches, or "jobs," in a biotic community are filled, extinction must occur as rapidly as the evolution of new species. The fossil record of the last ten million years bears witness to this fact, for it is replete with extinct animals that were sacrificed to make room for new and presumably superior species. But this is a normal state of affairs from a paleontologist's point of view.

However, the extinction that took place at the end of the Pleistocene did not comply with biological rules of survival. Unlike former extinctions, such as occurred in the Miocene, Pliocene, and Early Pleistocene, Late Pleistocene extinction of large mammals far exceeded replacement by new species that could easily have been accommodated by the prevailing habitat. The complete removal of North American horses, for example, represents the loss of a lineage of grass-eaters, without the loss of the grass! It left the horse niche empty for at least eight thousand years, until the Spaniards introduced Old World horses and burros. Some of these then escaped to reoccupy part of their prehistoric range. Today, tens of thousands of wild horses and burros still live along remote parts of the Colorado River and in the wild lands of the West. Certainly nothing happened at the end of the Pleistocene to destroy horse habitat. What, then, caused these animals, not to mention mammoths, camels, sloths, and others, to become extinct?

Like the horses, camels first evolved in North America many millions of years ago. They then spread into South America and crossed to the Old World by means of the Bering bridge. Crossing in the opposite direction were elephants, which soon prospered in the New World, judging by the abundance of mammoth and mastodon teeth in Pleistocene outcrops. From their evolutionary center in South America came a variety of edentates, including ground sloths and glyptodonts, the former spreading north to Alaska. But by the end of the Pleistocene, the majority of these herbivorous species had completely disappeared. Only relatively small species within these groups survived—the alpaca and llama among the camels of South America, and the relatively small edentates such as anteaters, armadillos, and tree sloths.

There was no obvious ecological substitution by other large herbivores competing for the same resources. Too many large mammals were lost, too few were replaced, and there was too little change among smaller plants and animals to accept this extinction as a normal event in the process of North American mammalian evolution.

One hypothesis commonly proposed for the abrupt and almost simultaneous extinction of large mammals is that of sudden climatic change. We know that climates did change many times in the Pleistocene—a three-million-year period of repeated glacial advance and retreat—so perhaps the great herds were decimated in this way. A sizable group of vertebrate paleontologists believe that that is indeed what happened. They maintain that with the retreat of the glaciers the early postglacial climate grew more continental—summers became hotter, and winters colder and supposedly more severe than they had been during the time of the ice advance. The result was an upset in the breeding season, a lethal cold sterility imposed on species of large mammals adapted for reproduction at what came to be the wrong season. Perhaps also the large Ice Age mammals were confronted for the first time with excessive snow cover and blue northers, which even today can kill thousands of cattle and sheep in the High Plains. Paleozoologist John Guilday at the Carnegie Museum believes that accelerated competition occurred among the large mammals before they could readjust to the change in vegetation and climate. They proceeded to exterminate their food supply and themselves in a morbid togetherness. Then, according to Guilday, the early North American hunters who arrived over the Bering bridge delivered the coup de grâce to the few remaining large mammals after the great herds were already sadly depleted.

But we have no evidence that the large mammals were under competitive stress, then or at any other time in the Pleistocene. We know that they had witnessed, and certainly survived, the advance and retreat of earlier glacial ice sheets. And among today's large mammals most are remarkably tolerant of different types of environments. Some large desert mammals can endure months without drinking; others, such as musk ox, live the year round in the high Arctic. Reindeer and wildebeest migrate hundreds of miles to pick their pasture. Why should we believe that the great mammals of the Pleistocene were less adaptable?

Furthermore, while climatic changes had some effect upon existing fauna and its habitat, extinction apparently occurred when range conditions were actually improving for many species. From the fossil pollen record we know that mastodon and woodland musk ox of eastern North America occupied spruce forests ten to twelve thousand years ago, a habitat then rapidly expanding northward from its constricted position bordering the Wisconsin ice sheet. And the western plains grassland was extensive and spreading at the time of the extinction of grazing horses, mammoths, and antelopes.

Another objection to cold winter climates as an explanation for extinction arises when one looks to the American Tropics. There, far more species became extinct during this period than in the temperate regions. More extinct Pleistocene genera were found in a single fauna in Bolivia than are known in the richest of the fossil faunas of the United States. However, the Tropics never experienced the zero temperatures of North America. This being the case, the climatic change hypothesis cannot account for the large-scale extinction in that part of the world.

Nor can it account for the extinction that occurred on the large islands of the world, such as on Madagascar and New Zealand, which did not take place until less than a thousand years ago. In the case of the giant bird, *Aepyornis,* of Madagascar, and the giant moa from New Zealand, carbon 14 dates indicate that these birds did not perish until long after the time of major worldwide climatic upset.

Without doubt, the climatic disturbances that affected North America during the Pleistocene proved equally distrubing in New Zealand. During the last glaciation one third of the South Island was ice covered and the remainder of the island was much colder than today. The subsequent melting of the glaciers brought a worldwide rise in sea level and divided the country in two. During the post-glacial period intense volcanic eruptions blanketed the North Island, so that by 2,000 years ago large parts of it were covered by sterile ash supporting only dwarfed vegetation. In fact, sheep raising failed in these areas until cobalt and other trace elements were added to the pastures. Yet, some 27 species of moas apparently survived the natural climatic catastrophes of the Pleistocene and disappeared only after East Polynesian invaders, the predecessors of the Maori, arrived sometime about or before A.D. 900. Thus, any credibility the climatic change hypothesis may have when applied to a single region vanishes when the global pattern is considered. Pleistocene experts generally believe that whatever their magnitude, major climatic changes of the last 50,000 years occurred at approximately the same time throughout the world—the extinctions did not.

My own hypothesis is that man, and man alone, was responsible for the unique wave of Late Pleistocene extinction—a case of overkill rather than "overchill" as implied by the climatic change theory. This view is neither new nor widely held, but when examined on a global basis, in which Africa, North America, Australia, Eurasia, and the islands of the world are considered, the pattern and timing of large-scale extinction corresponds to only one event—the arrival of prehistoric hunters.

Some anthropologists, such as Loren Eiseley of the University of Pennsylvania, have challenged the man-caused extinction theory on the grounds that

African megafauna did not suffer the same fate as the large mammals of North America. At first, this appears to be a sound argument since that continent now contains some 40 genera of large mammals that were around during the Pleistocene. Africa's fabulous plains fauna has long been regarded as a picture of what the American Pleistocene was like prior to extinction, at least in terms of size and diversity of the big mammals. During the million years of hominid evolution in Africa, it seems as if man and his predecessors would have had ample time to exterminate its fauna. And if, as I believe, Late Paleolithic hunters in the New World could have succeeded in destroying more than 100 species of large mammals in a period of only 1,000 years, then African hunters, it seems, should at least have made a dent on that continent's mammals.

It turns out that they did, for today's living megafauna in Africa represents only about 70 percent of the species that were present during the Late Pleistocene. Thus, while the proportion of African mammals that perished during the Pleistocene was less than that in North America, the loss in number of species was still considerable. In addition to the large mammals that now inhabit the African continent, an imaginary Pleistocene game park would have been stocked with such species as the antlered giraffe, a number of giant pigs, the stylohipparion horse, a great long-horned buffalo, a giant sheep, and an ostrich of larger size than is known at present. In Africa, as in America, the wave of Pleistocene extinction took only the large animals.

The African extinction has also been attributed to climatic and climate-related change. L. S. B. Leakey would explain extinction of the giant African fauna as the result of drought. If so, the drought strangely did not affect nearby Madagascar. On that island, barely 250 miles from the African shore, extinction of giant lemurs, pygmy hippopotamuses, giant birds, and tortoises did not occur until a much later date, in fact not until within the last 1,000 years.

African big game extinction appears to coincide in time with the first record of fire, or at least of charcoal, in archeological sites. In addition, most extinct fauna is last found in many locations associated with the distinctive stone tools of Early Stone Age (Acheulean) hunters. If fire was used in hunting, man-caused extinction becomes easier to understand, because fire drives necessarily involve large amounts of waste—whole herds must be decimated in order to kill the few animals sought for food. Perhaps fire became a major weapon in the hands of the Acheulean big game hunters, enabling them to encircle whole herds of animals.

In any event, African extinction ended during the period of the Early Stone Age hunters. This fact raises the possibility that the cultures that succeeded the Acheulean developed more selective methods of hunting and may even have learned to harvest the surviving large mammals on a sustained yield basis. Even during the last 100 years, when modern weapons have reduced the ranges of many species, there has been no loss of whole genera of terrestrial mammals, as occurred during the time of the early hunters.

The case of Australia also supports the hypothesis of man-caused extinction.

On that continent, no evidence of extinction, without replacement by other species, can be found until after men had inhabited the island, at least 14,000 years ago. About this time, various species of large marsupials perished, including the rhino-sized *Diprotodon* and the giant kangaroo.

About 12,000 years ago, when the Paleo-Indians swept into North America across the Bering bridge, through unglaciated Alaska, and down the melting ice corridor east of the Cordilleras, we can be confident that they were old hands at hunting woolly mammoths and other large Eurasian mammals. In contrast, the New World mammoth and other species of big game had never encountered man, and were unprepared for escaping the strange two-legged creature who used fire and stone-tipped spears to hunt them in communal bands. Probably the New World fauna of the time was no more suspicious of man than are the fearless animals that now live in the Galápagos and other regions uninhabited by men. In any case, radio-carbon dates indicate that North American extinction followed very closely on the heels of the big game hunters. The Paleo-Indians easily found and hunted the gregarious species that ranged over the grasslands, deserts, or other exposed habitat. As the hunters increased in number and spread throughout the continent, large animals whose low rate of reproduction was insufficient to offset the sudden burden of supporting a "superpredator" soon perished. . . .

Can the overkill hypothesis be disproved by future experiments or discoveries? To discount the hypothesis one need simply indentify a major wave of extinction anywhere in the world in the Late Pleistocene prior to man's arrival. To date, such evidence has not been found. Quite the opposite, in fact, since the chronological sequence of extinction follows closely upon man's footsteps—occurring first in Africa and southern Asia, next in Australia, then through northern Eurasia and into North and South America, much later in the West Indies, and finally, during the last 1,000 years, in Madagascar and New Zealand. The pattern shows that Late Pleistocene extinction did not occur in all locations at the same time, as it would have if there had been a sudden climatic change or perhaps a cataclysmic destruction of the earth's atmosphere with lethal radiation caused by cosmic ray bombardment, another common hypothesis. Since no synchronous destruction of plants or of plant communities is known, the long-held belief that climatic change caused extinction lacks credibility.

I do not pretend that the overkill hypothesis explains how, why, or even how many early hunters were involved. It seems reasonable to assume that fire and fire drives were a major weapon; possibly plant poisons were used in the Tropics. To the objection that too few spear points or other Stone Age artifacts have been found in the Americas to prove there was a sizable prehistoric human population, one may assert, tongue in cheek, that too few fossils of Pleistocene ground sloths, mammoths, camels, and saber-toothed cats have been found to prove there was a sizable prehistoric population of them either. The obvious difficulty with the "spear point" argument is that even the best fossil localities, with or without artifacts, do not yield data that can be reliably converted into population estimates. The case for overkill is best presented as a "least improbable hypothesis," and is not based on extensive knowledge of how prehistoric hunters may have carried out their hunting. Nor is there much hope that we will ever learn more of their techniques than the little we now know. The essence of the argument is based upon the simple matter of Late Pleistocene chronology. In no part of the world does massive unbalanced faunal extinction occur without man the hunter on the scene.

To certain comfortable concepts about pristine wilderness and ancient man, the implications of this hypothesis are startling, even revolutionary. For example, that business of the noble savage, a child of nature, living in an unspoiled Garden of Eden until the "discovery" of the New World by Europeans is apparently untrue, since the destruction of fauna, if not of habitat, was far greater before Columbus than at any time since. The subtle lesson of sustained yields, of not killing the goose that lays the golden eggs, may have been learned the hard way, and forgotten, many times before the twentieth century.

Rachel Carson

Silent Spring

From all over the world come echoes of the peril that faces birds in our modern world. The reports differ in detail, but always repeat the theme of death to wildlife in the wake of pesticides. Such are the stories of hundreds of small birds and partridges dying in France after vine stumps were treated with an arsenic-containing herbicide, or of partridge shoots in Belgium, once famous for the numbers of their birds, denuded of partridges after the spraying of nearby farmlands.

In England the major problem seems to be a specialized one, linked with the growing practice of treating seed with insecticides before sowing. Seed treatment is not a wholly new thing, but in earlier years the chemicals principally used were fungicides. No effects on birds seem to have been noticed. Then about 1956 there was a change to dual-purpose treatment; in addition to a fungicide, dieldrin, aldrin, or heptachlor was added to combat soil insects. Thereupon the situation changed for the worse.

In the spring of 1960 a deluge of reports of dead birds reached British wildlife authorities, including the British Trust for Ornithology, the Royal Society for the Protection of Birds, and the Game Birds Association. "The place is like a battlefield," a landowner in Norfolk wrote. "My keeper has found innumerable corpses, including masses of small birds—Chaffinches, Greenfinches, Linnets, Hedge

Sparrows, also House Sparrows . . . the destruction of wild life is quite pitiful." A gamekeeper wrote: "My Partridges have been wiped out with the dressed corn, also some Pheasants and all other birds, hundreds of birds have been killed. . . . As a lifelong gamekeeper it has been a distressing experience for me. It is bad to see pairs of Partridges that have died together."

In a joint report, the British Trust for Ornithology and the Royal Society for the Protection of Birds described some 67 kills of birds—a far from complete listing of the destruction that took place in the spring of 1960. Of these 67, 59 were caused by seed dressings, 8 by toxic sprays.

A new wave of poisoning set in the following year. The death of 600 birds on a single estate in Norfolk was reported to the House of Lords, and 100 pheasants died on a farm in North Essex. It soon became evident that more counties were involved than in 1960 (34 compared with 23). Lincolnshire, heavily agricultural, seemed to have suffered most, with reports of 10,000 birds dead. But destruction involved all of agricultural England, from Angus in the north to Cornwall in the south, from Anglesey in the west to Norfolk in the east.

In the spring of 1961 concern reached such a peak that a special committee of the House of Commons made an investigation of the matter, taking testimony from farmers, landowners, and representatives of the Ministry of Agriculture and of various governmental and nongovernmental agencies concerned with wildlife.

"Pigeons are suddenly dropping out of the sky dead," said one witness. "You can drive a hundred or two hundred miles outside London and not see a single kestrel," reported another. "There has been no parallel in the present century, or at any time so far as I am aware, [this is] the biggest risk to wildlife and game that ever occurred in the country," officials of the Nature Conservancy testified.

Facilities for chemical analysis of the victims were most inadequate to the task, with only two chemists in the country able to make the tests (one the government chemist, the other in the employ of the Royal Society for the Protection of Birds). Witnesses described huge bonfires on which the bodies of the birds were burned. But efforts were made to have carcasses collected for examination, and of the birds analyzed, all but one contained pesticide residues. The single exception was a snipe, which is not a seed-eating bird.

Along with the birds, foxes also may have been affected, probably indirectly by eating poisoned mice or birds. England, plagued by rabbits, sorely needs the fox as a predator. But between November 1959 and April 1960 at least 1300 foxes died. Deaths were heaviest in the same counties from which sparrow hawks, kestrels, and other birds of prey virtually disappeared, suggesting that the poison was spreading through the food chain, reaching out from the seed eaters to the furred and feathered carnivores. The actions of the moribund foxes were those of animals poisoned by chlorinated hydrocarbon insecticides. They were seen wandering in circles, dazed and half blind, before dying in convulsions.

The hearings convinced the committee that the threat to wildlife was "most alarming"; it accordingly recommended to the House of Commons that "the Minister of Agriculture and the Secretary of State for Scotland should secure the immediate prohibition for the use as seed dressings of compounds containing dieldrin, aldrin, or heptachlor, or chemicals of comparable toxicity." The committee also recommended more adequate controls to ensure that chemicals were adequately tested under field as well as laboratory conditions before being put on the market. This, it is worth emphasizing, is one of the great blank spots in pesticide research everywhere. Manufacturers' tests on the common laboratory animals—rats, dogs, guinea pigs—include no wild species, no birds as a rule, no fishes, and are conducted under controlled and artificial conditions. Their application to wildlife in the field is anything but precise.

England is by no means alone in its problem of protecting birds from treated seeds. Here in the United States the problem has been most troublesome in the rice-growing areas of California and the South. For a number of years California rice growers have been treating seed with DDT as protection against tadpole shrimp and scavenger beetles which sometimes damage seedling rice. California sportsmen have enjoyed excellent hunting because of the concentrations of waterfowl and pheasants in the rice fields. But for the past decade persistent reports of bird losses, especially among pheasants, ducks, and blackbirds, have come from the rice-growing counties. "Pheasant sickness" became a well-known phenomenon: birds "seek water, become paralyzed, and are found on the ditch banks and rice checks quivering," according to one observer. The "sickness" comes in the spring, at the time the rice fields are seeded. The concentration of DDT used is many times the amount that will kill an adult pheasant.

The passage of a few years and the development of even more poisonous insecticides served to increase the hazard from treated seed. Aldrin, which is 100 times as toxic as DDT to pheasants, is now widely used as a seed coating. In the rice fields of eastern Texas, this practice has seriously reduced the populations of the fulvous tree duck, a tawny-colored, gooselike duck of the Gulf Coast. Indeed, there is some reason to think that the rice growers, having found a way to reduce the populations of blackbirds, are using the insecticide for a dual purpose, with disastrous effects on several bird species of the rice fields.

As the habit of killing grows—the resort to "eradicating" any creature that may annoy or inconvenience us—birds are more and more finding themselves a direct target of poisons rather than an incidental one. There is a growing trend toward aerial applications of such deadly poisons as parathion to "control" concentrations of birds distasteful to farmers. The Fish and Wildlife Service has found it necessary to express serious concern over this trend, pointing out that "parathion treated areas constitute a potential hazard to humans, domestic animals, and wildlife." In southern Indiana, for example, a group of farmers went together in the summer of 1959 to engage a spray plane to treat an area of river bottomland with parathion. The area was a favored roosting site for thousands of blackbirds that were feeding in nearby cornfields. The problem could have been solved easily by a slight change in agricultural practice—a shift to a variety of corn with deep-set ears not accessible to the birds—but the farmers had been persuaded of the merits of·killing by poison, and so they sent in the planes on their mission of death.

The results probably gratified the farmers, for the casualty list included some 65,000 red-winged blackbirds and starlings. What other wildlife deaths may have gone unnoticed and unrecorded is not known. Parathion is not a specific for black-birds: it is a universal killer. But such rabbits or raccoons or opossums as may have roamed those bottomlands and perhaps never visited the farmers' cornfields were doomed by a judge and jury who neither knew of their existence nor cared.

And what of human beings? In California orchards sprayed with this same parathion, workers handling foliage that had been treated *a month* earlier collapsed and went into shock, and escaped death only through skilled medical attention. Does Indiana still raise any boys who roam through woods or fields and might even explore the margins of a river? If so, who guarded the poisoned area to keep out any who might wander in, in misguided search for unspoiled nature? Who kept vigilant watch to tell the innocent stroller that the fields he was about to enter were deadly—all their vegetation coated with a lethal film? Yet at so fearful a risk the farmers, with none to hinder them, waged their needless war on blackbirds.

In each of these situations, one turns away to ponder the question: Who has made the decision that sets in motion these chains of poisonings, this ever-widening wave of death that spreads out, like ripples when a pebble is dropped into a still pond? Who has placed in one pan of the scales the leaves that might have been eaten by the beetles and in the other the pitiful heaps of many-hued feathers, the lifeless remains of the birds that fell before the unselective bludgeon of insecticidal poisons? Who has decided—who has the *right* to decide—for the countless legions of people who were not consulted that the supreme value is a world without insects, even though it be also a sterile world ungraced by the curving wing of a bird in flight? The decision is that of the authoritarian temporarily entrusted with power; he has made it during a moment of inattention by millions to whom beauty and the ordered world of nature still have a meaning that is deep and imperative.

4
The Blight of Urban Life

Through the centuries the city has come to be the center of human activity and the symbol of human achievement. The city is an artificially created environment, a drastic alteration of nature in which human beings crowd together in unnatural circumstances that magnify the problems of disposal of human waste in its many forms. This has been the character of cities since ancient times. Because of the density of population, city dwellers have been encumbered with onerous burdens created by sewage disposal, garbage collection, air pollution, water contamination, and the general dehumanization of living conditions. The gathering into cities was undoubtedly a key step in the civilizing process, perhaps the most critical prerequisite to civilization. Paradoxically, it was also a key step in the creation of the ecological dilemma of urban blight. The enormous success of the modern city has been accompanied by life for millions in concrete and asphalt prisons filled with too many people and too much smog, trash, noise, and violence.

 The problems with which people have had to contend in the urban environment are examined in this section. The initial selections offer descriptions of conditions in cities in the ancient and medieval eras. These cities were perplexed by the same things that exercise urban areas today: excessive crowding and disposal of waste. Although its plight was not of the magnitude of modern urban devastation, it is clear that even the fabulous ancient city of Rome had to cope with awesome conditions of urban squalor. For its time early Rome enjoyed highly developed public utilities. Drainage was provided through a sophisticated network of sewers, and water was diverted into the city through a system of aqueducts that stands as a monument to Roman engineering skill. Nonetheless, the Romans had a horrendous problem of sewage collection and disposal. Ancient Rome had a maximum population of some one million people occupying an area roughly equivalent to that of Disneyland. By the first century A.D. sewage disposal had become critical to the health and proper functioning of this crowded metropolis. But virtually insurmountable obstacles existed, especially in the numerous "insula" or multi-level apartment houses that had no facilities for waste disposal on the upper floors. Jérôme Carcopino gives a vivid description of the nature of Roman sanitation facilities in a city with crowded slums, unhealthy public toilets, and inadequate provision for liquidating waste.

While early Rome rivaled many modern cities in population, the towns of medieval Europe were quite small. But like Rome, the disposal of waste matter taxed the technology of the infant cities of the Middle Ages. Judging from the descriptions by Urban Holmes and by Joseph and Frances Gies, no satisfactory solutions existed beyond dumping refuse and human waste into the nearest river. Holmes' observations depict the deficient sewage facilities in the homes and streets of twelfth-century Paris and London. The Gies' account of street life in a thirteenth-century French commercial district and the resultant pollution of the Vienne River from the wastes of tanners, butchers, and other craftsmen suggests that the medieval answer to waste disposal problems resembled the approach later employed in industrialized cities: get the waste into the rivers and out of the immediate vicinity as quickly as possible. Clearly the unpleasant, unhealthy, and crowded conditions that menace modern cities have their counterparts in ancient and medieval Europe.

The premodern cities, however, did not present genuine threats to the world environment. Urban devastation created an unattractive environment for the people cramped into the cities amid filth, but it was only with the industrial revolution that the city began to leave permanent damage in its wake and to challenge the total environment. As people ransacked the mineral wealth of the Earth on a grand scale, leaving lasting scars, they also flocked to the cities where they magnified the ecological problems of their ancestors many times over. Lewis Mumford offers an excellent description of the impact of industrialism—coal mines, iron and steel works, railroads, and mass labor exploitation—upon the city. The factory town, offspring of unlimited use of fossil fuels, the steam engine, and rampant capitalism, produced an entirely new urban environment. The crude, coal-smudged factory agglomerations of the nineteenth century, into which human beings were packed like so many parts of the machines they served, were incalculably more damaging to the natural environment and to the people themselves then had been ancient Rome or the feudal villages of the Middle Ages. Mumford presents a view of the industrial "Coketown," its air thick with coal smoke belching from noisy locomotives and bleak mill stacks, its rivers slimy with industrial sludge and human waste, its people living in unsightly brick houses amid slag heaps, rail yards, and dingy factories.

In *Hard Times* Charles Dickens has left us a classic portrait of the English industrial city of the mid-nineteenth century that reveals the glaring reality of the

sombre life created by mechanization and mass industrialism. In his fictional account, Dickens intimates that the factory town had a dehumanizing effect upon its
inhabitants. George Carstairs would agree that the conditions of crowding, filth,
and pollution operative in Coketown probably had a tremendous impact upon the
lives of people caught up in that morass of urban-industrial blight. Carstairs maintains that similar conditions of overcrowding in the slums of modern cities may be
taking a comparable human toll. He finds historical and scientific evidence to indicate that overcrowding in cities encourages uncertain, frustrating circumstances
which lead to extremely aggressive human behavior. Overcrowding of animals and
humans alike appears to aggravate social instability which, in turn, breeds violence.
The psychological effect of urban crowding seems to manifest itself in mental disorder and pathologically belligerent activity, and Carstairs suggests a tie between
crimes of violence and congested urban living. Perhaps overcrowding breeds human
aggression just as stuffing too many rats into a cage causes them to act violently.

The impact of modern industrialized urban areas upon the total environment
is stupendous. The problems of waste disposal experienced by ancient and medieval
Europeans are minuscule when compared to those of the fabulous factory-cities of
the mid-twentieth century. Michael Drapkin and Thomas Ehrich, staff reporters for
the *Wall Street Journal,* give some insight into the polluting effect of the cities
along the Ohio River in America's industrial heartland. For two centuries the min-
eral-rich Ohio basin has witnessed the growth of more and larger industrialized
cities. The growth in population has been paralleled by an increase in human and
industrial effluent that has been dumped into the convenient Ohio River, turning it
into a giant oozing cesspool filled with lumps of raw sewage and factory sludge.
Even Dickens' Coketown could not match the pollution of the "dirty Ohio."

In a brief historical sketch of air pollution, Leslie Chambers shows that as
early as the thirteenth century the English were aware of the obnoxious qualities
of burning coal. And the Coketowns of the nineteenth century pumped the atmosphere full of smoke and soot on a scale never realized in preindustrial society. In
the past century smog has descended upon the great urban-industrial complexes of
the world like a visitation of deadly mist. The final selection of this section, by
Robert and Leona Rienow, drives home with frightening clarity the fact that the
air in modern industrial cities is unfit for healthful human existence. The Rienows
report that each day the average New Yorker breaths in the toxic equivalent of
almost two packs of cigarettes because the city's atmosphere serves as the dumping
ground for thousands of tons of airborne garbage. The problems are the same in
New York as they were in Coketown a century ago, only they have been magnified
to catastrophic proportions. As industrial progress continues, ecological problems
in cities become increasingly complex and solutions harder to achieve. Now urban-
ites find themselves drowning in the filth that is a by-product of their own genius.

Jérôme Carcopino

Living Conditions
in Ancient Rome

The praetorian prefect Paulus, in issuing instructions to the *praefectus vigilum,* did not forget to remind the commandant of the Roman firemen that it was part of his duty to warn tenants always to keep water ready in their rooms to check an outbreak. . . .

Obviously, if the Romans of imperial times had needed only to turn a tap and let floods of water flow into a sink, this warning would have been superfluous. The mere fact that Paulus expressly formulated the warning proves that, with a few exceptions [adequate quantities of fresh] water from the aqueducts reached only the ground floor of the *insula.* The tenants of the upper *cenacula* had to go and draw their water from the nearest fountain. The higher the flat was perched, the harder the task of carrying water to scrub the floors and walls of those crowded *contignationes.* It must be confessed that the lack of plentiful water for washing invited the tenants of many Roman *cenacula* to allow filth to accumulate, and it was inevitable that many succumbed to the temptation for lack of a water system such as never existed save in the imagination of too optimistic archaeologists.

Far be it from me to stint my well-deserved admiration for the network of sewers which conveyed the sewage of the city into the Tiber. The sewers of Rome were begun in the sixth century B.C. and continually extended and improved under the republic and under the empire. The *cloacae* were conceived, carried out, and kept up on so grandiose a scale that in certain places a wagon laden with hay could drive through them with ease; and Agrippa, who perhaps did more than any man to increase their efficiency and wholesomeness by diverting the overflow of the aqueducts into them through seven channels, had no difficulty in travelling their entire length by boat. They were so solidly constructed that the mouth of the largest, as well as the oldest of them, the *Cloaca Maxima,* the central collector for all the others from the Forum to the foot of the Aventine, can still be seen opening into the river at the level of the Ponte Rotto. Its semicircular arch, five metres in diameter, is as perfect today as in the days of the kings to whom it is attributed. Its patinated, tufa voussoirs have triumphantly defied the passage of twenty-five hundred years. It is a masterpiece in which the enterprise and patience of the Roman people collaborated with the long experience won by the Etruscans in the drainage of their marshes; and, such as it has come down to us, it does honor to antiquity.

But it cannot be denied that the ancients, though they were courageous enough to undertake it, and patient enough to carry it through, were not skillful enough to utilize it as we would have done in their place. They did not turn it to full account for securing a cleanly town or ensuring the health and decency of the inhabitants.

The system served to collect the sewage of the *rez-de-chausée* and of the public latrines which stood directly along the route, but no effort was made to connect the *cloacae* with the private latrines of the separate *cenacula.* There are only a few houses in Pompeii whose upstairs latrines were so designed that they could empty into the sewer below, whether by a conduit connecting them with the sewer or by a special arrangement of pipes, and the same can be said of Ostia and Herculaneum. But since this type of drainage is lacking in the most imposing *insulae* of Ostia as in those of Rome, we may abide in general by the judgment of Abbé Thédenat, who thirty-five years ago stated unequivocally that the living quarters of the *insulae* had never at any time been linked with the *cloacae* of the Urbs. The drainage system of the Roman house is merely a myth begotten of the complacent imagination of modern times. Of all the hardships endured by the inhabitants of ancient Rome, the lack of domestic drainage is the one which would be most severely resented by the Romans of today.

The very rich escaped the inconvenience. If they lived in their own *domus,* they had nothing to do but construct a latrine on the ground level. Water from the aqueducts might reach it and at worst, if it was too far distant from one of the sewers for the refuse to be swept away, the sewage could fall into a trench beneath. These cess trenches, like the one excavated near San Pietro in 1892, were neither very deep nor proof against seepage, and the manure merchants had acquired the right—probably under Vespasian—to arrange for emptying them. If the priviledged had their *domus* in an *insula,* they rented the whole of the ground floor and enjoyed the same advantage as in a private house. The poor, however, had a longer way to go. In any case they were forced to go outside their homes. If the trifling cost was not deterrent, they could pay for entry to one of the public latrines administered by the *conductores foricarum.* . . .

But the public latrines were not the resort of misers or of the very poor. These folk had no mind to enrich the *conductores foricarum* to the tune of even one as. They preferred to have recourse to the jars, skillfully chipped down for the purpose, which the fuller at the corner ranged in front of his workshop. He purchased permission for this from Vespasian, in consideration of a tax to which no odor clung, so as to secure gratis the urine necessary for his trade. Alternatively they clattered down the stairs to empty their chamber pots (*lasana*) and their commodes (*sellae pertusae*) into the vat or *dolium* placed under the well of the staircase. Or if perhaps this expedient had been forbidden by the landlord of their *insula,* they betook themselves to some neighboring dungheap. For in Rome of the Caesars, as in a badly kept hamlet of today, more than one alley stank with the pestilential odor of a cess trench *(lacus)* such as those which Cato the Elder during his censorship paved over when he cleaned the *cloacae* and led them under the Aventine. Such malodorous trenches were extant in the days of Cicero and Caesar;

Lucretius mentions them in his poem, *De rerum natura.* Two hundred years later, in the time of Trajan, they were still there. . . .

There were other poor devils who found their stairs too steep and the road to these dung pits too long, and to save themselves further trouble would empty the contents of their chamber pots from their heights into the streets. So much the worse for the passer-by who happened to intercept the unwelcome gift! Fouled and sometimes even injured, as in Juvenal's satire, he had no redress save to lodge a complaint against the unknown assailant; many passages of the *Digest* indicate that Roman jurists did not disdain to take cognisance of this offense, to refer the case to the judges, to track down the offender, and assess the damages payable to the victim. . . .

Our great cities are also shadowed by misery, stained by the uncleanness of our slums, dishonored by the vice they harbor. But at least the disease which gnaws at them is usually localized and confined to certain blighted quarters, whereas we get the impression that slums invaded every corner of Imperial Rome. Almost everywhere throughout the Urbs the *insulae* were the property of owners who had no wish to be concerned directly in their management and who leased out the upper stories to a promoter for five-year terms—in return for a rent at least equal to that of the ground-floor *domus.* This principal tenant who set himself to exploit the sub-letting of the *cenacula* had no bed of roses. He had to keep the place in repair, obtain tenants, keep the peace between them, and collect his quarterly payments on the year's rent. Not unnaturally he sought compensation for his worries and his risks by extorting enormous profits. Ever-rising rent is a subject of eternal lamentation in Roman literature.

In 153 B.C. an exiled king had to share a flat with an artist, a painter, in order to make ends meet. In Caesar's day the humblest tenant had to pay a rent of 2,000 sesterces ($80) a year. In the times of Domitian and of Trajan, one could have bought a fine estate at Sora or Frusino for the price of quarters in Rome. So intolerable was the burden of rent that the sub-tenants of the first lessee almost invariably had to sub-let in their turn every room in their *cenaculum* which they could possibly spare. Almost everywhere, the higher you went in a building, the more breathless became the overcrowding, the more sordid the promiscuity. If the *rez-de-chaussée* was divided into several *tabernae,* they were filled with artisans, shopkeepers and eating-house keepers, like those of the *insula* which Petronius describes. If it had been retained for the use of one privileged possessor, it was occupied by the retainers of the owner of the *domus.* But whatever the disposition of the ground floor, the upper stories were gradually swamped by the mob: entire families were herded together in them; dust, rubbish, and filth accumulated; and finally bugs ran riot to such a point that one of the shady characters of Petronius' *Satyricon,* hiding under his miserable pallet, was driven to press his lips against the bedding which was black with them. Whether we speak of the luxurious and elegant *domus* or of the *insulae*—caravanserais whose heterogeneous inhabitants needed an army of slaves and porters under the command of a servile steward to keep order among them—the dwelling-houses of the Urbs were seldom ranged in order along an avenue, but jostled each other in a labyrinth of steep streets and lanes, all more or less narrow, tortuous, and dark, and the marble of the "palaces" shone in the obscurity of cut-throat alleys.

Urban T. Holmes, Jr.

Medieval Sanitation: I

The problem of locating the latrine was a serious one. Such a convenience was called a *longaigne,* which is to be translated "far-off place." Obviously the house-holders wished to isolate such a chamber, even though their limited space made it difficult. In the *Life of St. Gregory* the latrine is spoken of as a retiring place where tablets could be read without interruption. I am inclined to think that where the space permitted a *garde-robe* pit was dug apart from the house and a shed and wooden platform were placed over it. The Assise of 1189 in London demanded that such a pit should not be less than two and one-half feet from the property line. Boccaccio's *Decamerone* tells of an outdoor platform that collapsed under the occupant. This platform, however, was built in very unsanitary fashion over an open court. In some town houses the latrine must have been placed in the inner sleeping apartment, off from the main *salle,* with a chute provided to a pit in the floor of the cellar. This shaft would have an opening into the cellar through which it could be emptied. Words spoken above in the sleeping apartment would have an uncanny habit of being heard in the cellar as they drifted down the shaft. The ideal arrangement, practiced in a royal palace or a wealthy household, as in the halls attached to the royal castle at Salisbury, was to have a special latrine tower to which a door opened off from the *salle* or from an anteroom. Any small house so provided was indeed lucky. I am afraid that more often the waste pit near the kitchen fire took care of sewage as well as kitchen refuse. . . .

Although streams of water were encouraged to flow down the middle of the streets, there was a shortage of drainage ditches for these to empty into. Fortunately many of the Paris streets sloped toward the river, or toward the Bièvre. Drainage must have been remarkably bad on the Cité itself—in the royal palace and in the Cloister of Notre Dame. A ditch that was dug remained open to the air. Filth found its way constantly into the muddy streets. Chamber pots and washbasins could be emptied too by pitching the contents from the window. To avoid such

From *Daily Living in the Twelfth Century* by Urban T. Holmes, Jr. (Madison: The University of Wisconsin Press; © 1964 by the Regents of the University of Wisconsin), pp. 96-97, 101. Reprinted by permission.

foulness on a dry day, and the rushing gutter on a wet day, many rode through the
streets on horseback, and the others used heavy shoes with very high, thick soles.
The *chape* was a protection from water thrown from above. (It is easy to recognize
the origins of our modern polite rule that a gentleman should walk on the outside
while the lady takes the wall.)

Joseph Gies and Frances Gies

Medieval Sanitation: II

Two main thoroughfares [of Troyes] run east and west in the commercial section—
the Rue de l'Epicerie, which changes its name several times before it reaches the
canal, and to the north the Grande Rue, leading from the Porte de Paris to the
bridge that crosses into the old city. It is thirty feet wide and paved with stone. The
Grande Rue is appreciably broader and straighter than the side streets, where riders
and even pedestrians sometimes must squeeze past each other. The Ruelle des
Chats—"Cats' Alley"—is seven feet wide. Even on the Grande Rue one has a sense
of buildings crowding in, the three- and four-story frame houses and shops shoulder-
ing into the street, their corbelled upper stories looming irregularly above. Façades
are painted red and blue, or faced with tile, often ornamented with paneling, mold-
ings, and sawtooth. Colorful signboards hang over the doors of taverns, and trades-
men's symbols identify the shops. The shops open to the street, the lowered fronts
of their stalls serving as display counters for merchandise—boots, belts, purses,
knives, spoons, pots and pans, paternosters (rosaries). Inside, shopkeepers and
apprentices are visible at work.

Most traffic is on foot—artisans in bright-colored tunics and hose, housewives
in gowns and mantles, their hair covered by white wimples, merchants in fur-
trimmed coats, here and there the black or brown habit of a priest or monk. Honk-
ing geese flutter from under the hooves of horses. Dogs and cats lurk in the door-
ways or forage for food with the pigeons.

The streets have been freshly cleaned for the fair, but the smells of the city
are still present. Odors of animal dung and garbage mingle with pleasanter aromas
from cookshops and houses. The most pungent districts are those of the fish merchants, the linen makers, the butchers and, worst of all, the tanners. In the previous
century the expanding business of the tanners and butchers resulted in a typical

urban problem. The bed of the Vienne became choked with refuse. Count Henry the Generous had a canal dug from the upper Seine, increasing the flow into the Vienne and flushing out the pollution. But the butchers' and tanners' district remains the most undesirable neighborhood in town. Cities such as Troyes legislate to make householders and shopkeepers clean the streets in front of their houses, and to forbid emptying waste water into the streets. But such ordinances are only half effective. Rain compounds the problem by turning the unpaved streets to mud. . . .

Shoppers must watch their step in the streets, which are full of unpleasant surprises. In the butchers' quarter slaughtering is performed on the spot, and blood dries in the sun amid piles of offal and swarms of flies. Outside the poulterers' shops geese, tied to the aprons of the stalls, honk and gabble. Chickens and ducks, their legs trussed, flounder on the ground, along with rabbits and hares.

Lewis Mumford

The Impact of Industrialism

Up to the nineteenth century, there had been a rough balance of activities within the city. Though work and trade were always important, religion and art and play claimed their full share of the townsman's energies. But the tendency to concentrate on economic activities, and to regard as waste the time or effort spent on other functions, at least outside the home, had been growing steadily since the sixteenth century. If capitalism tended to expand the province of the marketplace and turn every part of the city into a negotiable commodity, the change from organized urban handicraft to large scale factory production transformed the industrial towns into dark hives, busily puffing, clanking, screeching, smoking for twelve and fourteen hours a day, sometimes going around the clock. The slavish routine of the mines, whose labor was an intentional punishment for criminals, became the normal environment of the new industrial worker. . . .

Between 1820 and 1900 the destruction and disorder within great cities is like that of a battlefield, proportionate to the very extent of their equipment and the strength of the forces employed. In the new provinces of city building, one must now keep one's eyes on the bankers, industrialists, and the mechanical inventors. They were responsible for most of what was good and almost all that was bad.

In their own image, they created a new type of city: that which Dickens, in *Hard Times,* called Coketown. In a greater or lesser degree, every city in the Western World was stamped with the archetypal characteristics of Coketown. Industrialism, the main creative force of the nineteenth century, produced the most degraded urban environment the world had yet seen; for even the quarters of the ruling classes were befouled and overcrowded. . . .

Villages expanded into towns; towns became metropolises. The number of urban centers multiplied; the number of cities with populations above five hundred thousand increased, too. Extraordinary changes of scale took place in the masses of buildings and the areas they covered: vast structures were erected almost overnight. Men built in haste, and had hardly time to repent of their mistakes before they tore down their original structures and built again, just as heedlessly. The newcomers, babies or immigrants, could not wait for new quarters: they crowded into whatever was offered. It was a period of vast urban improvisation: makeshift hastily piled upon makeshift.

Mark that the rapid growth of cities was no mere New World phenomenon. Indeed, the rate of city growth was swifter in Germany after 1870, when the paleotechnic revolution was in full swing there, than in new countries like the United States: this despite the fact that the United States was then steadily receiving immigrants. Though the nineteenth century was the first to rival the early Middle Ages in large scale land colonization and settlement, the premises upon which these enterprises were conducted were far more primitive than those of the eleventh century. Colonization by communities, except in the case of little idealistic groups, the most widely successful of which were the Mormons, was no longer the rule. Every man was for himself; and the Devil, if he did not take the hindmost, at least reserved for himself the privilege of building the cities.

Here in the new industrial centers was a chance to build on a firm foundation and make a fresh start: such a chance as democracy had in the eighteenth century claimed for itself in political government. Almost everywhere that opportunity was fumbled. In an age of technical progress the city, as a social and political unit, lay outside the circle of invention. Except for utilities such as gas mains, water pipes, and sanitary equipment, often belatedly introduced, often slipshod, always ill-distributed, the industrial city could claim no important improvements over the seventeenth-century town. Indeed, the most wealthy and "progressive" metropolises o often denied themselves elementary necessities of life like light and air that even backward villages still possessed. Until 1838 neither Manchester nor Birmingham even functioned politically as incorporated boroughs: they were man-heaps, machine-warrens, not agents of human association for the promotion of a better life. . . .

So immersed are we, even at this late date, in the surviving medium of paleotechnic beliefs that we are not sufficiently conscious of their profound abnormality. Few of us correctly evaluate the destructive imagery that the mine carried into every department of activity, sanctioning the anti-vital and the anti-organic. Before the nineteenth century the mine had, quantitatively speaking, only a subordinate part in man's industrial life. By the middle of the century it had come to underlie every part of it. And the spread of mining was accompanied by a general loss of form throughout society: a degradation of the landscape and a no less brutal disordering of the communal environment.

Agriculture creates a balance between wild nature and man's social needs. It restores deliberately what man subtracts from the earth; while the plowed field, the trim orchard, the serried vineyard, the vegetables, the grains, the flowers, are all examples of disciplined purpose, orderly growth, and beautiful form. The process of mining, on the other hand, is destructive: the immediate product of the mine is disorganized and inorganic; and what is once taken out of the quarry or the pithead cannot be replaced. Add to this the fact that continued occupation in agriculture brings cumulative improvements to the landscape and a finer adaptation of it to human needs; while mines as a rule pass quickly from riches to exhaustion, from exhaustion to desertion, often within a few generations. Mining thus presents the very image of human discontinuity, here today and gone tomorrow, now feverish with gain, now depleted and vacant.

From the eighteen-thirties on, the environment of the mine, once restricted to the original site, was universalized by the railroad. Wherever the iron rails went, the mine and its debris went with them. Whereas the canals of the eotechnic phase, with their locks and bridges and tollhouses, with their trim banks and their gliding barges, had brought a new element of beauty into the rural landscape, the railroads of the paleotechnic phase made huge gashes: the cuts and embankments for the greater part long remained unplanted, and the wound in the earth was unhealed. The rushing locomotives brought noise, smoke, grit, into the hearts of the towns: more than one superb urban site, like Prince's Gardens in Edinburgh, was desecrated by the invasion of the railroad. And the factories that grew up alongside the railroad sidings mirrored the slatternly environment of the railroad itself. If it was in the mining town that the characteristic process of *Abbau*—mining or unbuilding—was seen at its purest, it was by means of the railroad that this process was extended by the third quarter of the nineteenth century to almost every industrial community. . . .

But at the same time, an *Abbau,* or un-building, was taking place, often at an even more rapid rate, in other parts of the environment: forests were slaughtered, soils were mined, whole animal species, such as the beaver, the bison, the wild pigeon, were practically wiped out, while the sperm whales and right whales were seriously decimated. Therewith the natural balance of organisms within their ecological regions was upset, and a lower and simpler biological order—sometimes marked by the complete extermination of the prevalent forms of life—followed Western man's ruthless exploitation of nature for the sake of his temporary and socially limited profit economy. . . .

Humanly speaking, some of the worst features of the factory system, the long hours, the monotonous work, the low wages, the systematic misappropriation of child labor, had been established under the decentralized eotechnic organization of production. Exploitation began at home. But water power and canal transportation did little damage to the landscape; and mining and smelting, as long as they remained small in scale and scattered, made scars that were easily healed. Even today, in the Forest of Dean, near the Severn, where the ancient practices of charcoal burning mingle with those of small scale mining, the mining villages are more comely than in more "dynamic" areas, and both the mines and the slag heaps are easily hidden by trees or almost effaced by other vegetation. It was the change of scale, the unrestricted massing of populations and industries, that produced some of the most horrendous urban effects.

The use of Watt's steam engine as a prime mover, changed all this: particularly, it changed the scale and made feasible a far heavier concentration of both industries and workers, while it removed the worker himself farther from the rural base that gave the cottager with his garden an auxiliary supply of food and a touch of independence. The new fuel magnified the importance of the coal fields and fostered industry there or in places accessible by canal or railroad.

Steam worked most efficiently in big concentrated units, with the parts of the plant no more than a quarter of a mile from the power-center: every spinning machine or loom had to tap power from the belts and shafts worked by the central steam engine. The more units in a given area, the more efficient was the source of power: hence the tendency toward giantism. Big factories, such as those developed in Manchester, New Hampshire, from the eighteen-twenties onward—repeated in New Bedford and Fall River—could utilize the latest instruments of power production, whereas the smaller factories were at a technical disadvantage. A single factory might employ two hundred and fifty hands. A dozen such factories, with all the accessory instruments and services, were already the nucleus of a considerable town.

In their attempts to produce machine-made goods at low prices for consumption in the world market, the manufacturers cut costs at every point in order to increase profits. The most obvious place to begin this paring was in the wages of the workers. In the eighteenth century, as Robert Owen noted, even the most enlightened manufacturers made unsparing use of child labor and pauper labor: but when the age of child workers was legally regulated and the supply diminished, it became necessary to tap other sources. To have the necessary surplus of workers, to meet the extra demands in the busy seasons, it was important for industry to settle near a great center of population, for in a country village the support of the idle might fall directly upon the manufacturer himself, who often owned the cottages and might, during a shutdown, lose his rents.

It was the manic-depressive rhythm of the market, with its spurts and stoppages, that made the large urban center so important to industry. For it was by drawing at need on an underlayer of surplus labor, fitfully employed, that the new capitalists managed to depress wages and meet any sudden demand in production. Size, in other words, took the place of an efficiently organized labor market, with union wage standards and public employment exchanges. Topographical agglomeration was a substitute for a well-timed and humanely regulated mode of production, such as has been coming into existence the last half-century.

If the steam-powered factory, producing for the world market, was the first factor that tended to increase the area of urban congestion, the new railroad transporation system, after 1830, greatly abetted it.

Power was concentrated on the coal fields. Where coal could be mined or obtained by cheap means of transportation, industry could produce regularly throughout the year without stoppages through seasonal failure of power. In a business system based upon time-contracts and time-payments, this regularity was highly important. Coal and iron thus exercised a gravitational pull on many subsidiary and accessory industries: first by means of the canal, and after 1830, through the new railroads. A direct connection with the mining areas was a prime condition of urban concentration: until our own day the chief commodity carried by the railroads was coal for heat and power. . . .

Population growth, then, during the paleotechnic regime, showed two characteristic patterns: a general massing on the coal areas, where the new heavy industries, iron and coal mining, smelting, cutlery, hardware production, glass manufacture, and machine-building flourished. And in addition a partly derivative thickening of population along the new railroad lines, with a definite clotting in the industrial centers along the great trunk lines and a further massing in the greater junction towns and export terminals. . . .

The main elements in the new urban complex were the factory, the railroad, and the slum. By themselves they constituted the industrial town: a word that described merely the fact that more than two thousand people were gathered in an area that could be designated with a proper name. Such urban clots could and did expand a hundred times without acquiring more than a shadow of the institutions that characterize a city in the mature sociological sense—that is, a place in which the social heritage is concentrated, and in which the possibilities of continuous social intercourse and interaction raise to a higher potential all the complex activities of men. Except in shrunken, residual forms, even the characteristic organs of the stone age city were lacking.

The factory became the nucleus of the new urban organism. Every other detail of life was subordinate to it. Even the utilities, such as the water supply, and the minimum of governmental offices that were necessary to a town's existence often, if they had not been built by an earlier generation, entered belatedly: an afterthought. It was not merely art and religion that were treated by the utilitarian as mere embellishments: intelligent political administration long remained in the same category. In the first scramble of exploitation, no provisions would be made for police and fire protection, water and food inspection, hospital care, or education.

The factory usually claimed the best sites: mainly, in the cotton industry, the chemical industries, and the iron industries, the sites near a waterfront; for large quantities of water were needed now in the processes of production, supplying the steam boilers, cooling hot surfaces, making the necessary chemical solutions and dyes. Above all, the river or canal had still another important function: it was the cheapest and most convenient dumping ground for all soluble or suspendable forms of waste. The transformation of the rivers into open sewers was a characteristic feat of the new economy. Result: poisoning of the aquatic life: destruction of food: befouling of water so it was unfit to bathe in.

For generations, the members of every "progressive" urban community were forced to pay for the sordid convenience of the manufacturer, who often, it happened, consigned his precious by-products to the river, for lack of scientific knowledge or the empirical skill to use them. If the river was a liquid dump, great mounds of ashes, slag, rubbish, rusty iron, and even garbage blocked the horizon with their vision of misplaced and unusable matter. The rapidity of production was in part matched by the rapidity of consumption, and before a conservative policy of scrap metal utilization became profitable, the formless or deteriorated end-products were cast back over the surface of the landscape. In the Black Country of England, indeed, the huge slag heaps still look like geological formations: they decreased the available living space, cast a shadow on the land, and until recently presented an insoluble problem of either utilization or removal.

The testimony that substantiates this picture is voluminous; indeed, it is still open for inspection in the older industrial cities of the Western World, despite herculean efforts to cleanse the environment. Let me however quote from an early observer, Hugh Miller, the author of *Old Red Sandstone:* a man thoroughly in harmony with his age, but not insensitive to the actual qualities of the new environment. He is speaking of Manchester in 1862.

> Nothing seems more characteristic of the great manufacturing city, though disagreeably so, than the river Irwell, which runs through the place. . . . The hapless river—a pretty enough stream a few miles up, with trees overhanging its banks and fringes of green sedge set thick along its edges—loses caste as it gets among the mills and print works. There are myriads of dirty things given it to wash, and whole wagonloads of poisons from dye houses and bleachyards thrown into it to carry away; steam boilers discharge into it their seething contents, and drains and sewers their fetid impurities; till at length it rolls on—here between tall dingy walls, there under precipices of red sandstone—considerably less a river than a flood of liquid manure.

. . . While factories were usually set near the rivers, or the railroad lines that paralleled the rivers (except where a level terrain invited diffusion), no authority was exercised to concentrate factories in a particular area, to segregate the more noxious or noisy industries that should be placed far from human habitations, or to insulate for domestic purposes the appropriate adjacent areas. "Free competition" alone determined location, without thought of the possibility of functional planning: and the jumbling together of industrial, commercial, and domestic functions went on steadily in industrial cities.

In areas with a rough topography, such as the valleys of the Allegheny plateau, a certain amount of natural zoning might take place, since only the river bottoms would afford enough space for a big mill to spread—though this disposition ensured that the maximum amount of noxious effluvia would rise and spread over the homes on the hillsides above. Otherwise living quarters were often placed within the leftover spaces between the factories and sheds and the railroad yards. To pay attention to such matters as dirt, noise, vibration, was accounted an effeminate delicacy. Workers' houses, often those of the middle classes, too, would be built, smack up against a steel works, a dye plant, a gas works, or a railroad cutting. They would be built, often enough, on land filled in with ashes and broken glass and rubbish, where even the grass could not take root; they might be on the edge of a dump or a vast permanent pile of coal and slag: day in and day out the stench of the refuse, the murky outpouring of chimneys, the noise of hammering or of whirring machinery, accompanied the household routine.

In this new scheme, the town itself consisted of the shattered fragments of land, with odd shapes and inconsequential streets and avenues, left over between the factories, the railroads, the freight yards and dump heaps. In lieu of any kind of over-all municipal regulation or planning, the railroad itself was called upon to define the character and project the limits of the town. Except in certain parts of Europe where old-fashioned bureaucratic regulations happily kept the railroad stations at the outskirts of the historic city, the railroad was permitted, or rather, was invited to plunge into the very heart of the town and to create in the most precious central portions of the city a waste of freight yards and marshalling yards, economically justifiable only in the open country. These yards severed the town's natural arteries and created an impassable barrier between large urban segments: sometimes, as in Philadelphia, a veritable Chinese wall.

Thus the railroad carried into the heart of the city not merely noise and soot but the industrial plants and the debased housing that alone could thrive in the environment it produced. Only the hypnotism of a new invention, in an age uncritically enamored of new inventions, could have prompted this wanton immolation under the wheels of the puffing Juggernaut. Every mistake in urban design that could be made was made by the new railroad engineers, for whom the movement of trains was more important than the human objects achieved by that movement. The wastage of space by railroad yards in the heart of the city only furthered its more rapid extension outward; and this in turn, since it produced more railroad traffic, gave the extra sanction of profits to the misdemeanors so committed.

So widespread was this deterioration of environment, so hardened have people in big cities become to it in the course of a century, that even the richer classes, who could presumably afford the best, to this day often indifferently embrace the worst. As for housing itself, the alternatives were simple. In the industrial towns that grew up on older foundations, the workers were first accommodated by turning old one-family houses into rent barracks. In these made-over houses, each separate room would now enclose a whole family: from Dublin and Glasgow to Bombay, the standard of one room per family long held. Bed overcrowding, with three to eight people of different ages sleeping on the same pallet, often aggravated room overcrowding in such human sties. By the beginning of the nineteenth century, according to a Dr. Willan, who wrote a book on the diseases of London, it had produced an incredible state of physical defilement among the poor. The other type of dwelling offered to the working class was, essentially, a standardization of these degraded conditions; but it had this further defect, that the plans of the new houses and the materials of construction usually had none of the original decency of the older burgher houses: they were meanly built from the ground up.

In both the old and the new quarters a pitch of foulness and filth was reached that the lowest serf's cottage scarcely achieved in medieval Europe. It is almost impossible to enumerate objectively the bare details of this housing without being suspected of perverse exaggeration. But those who speak glibly of urban improvements during this period, or of the alleged rise in the standards of living, fight shy of the actual facts: they generously impute to the town as a whole benefits which only the more favored middle-class minority enjoyed; and they read into the original conditions those improvements which three generations of active legislation and massive sanitary engineering have finally brought about.

In England, to begin with, thousands of the new workers' dwellings, in towns like Birmingham and Bradford, were built back to back. (Many still exist.) Two rooms out of four on each floor therefore had no direct daylight or ventilation. There were no open spaces except the bare passages between these doubled rows. While in the sixteenth century it was an offense in many English towns to throw rubbish into the streets, in these early industrial towns this was the regular method of disposal. The rubbish remained there, no matter how vile and filthy, "until the accumulation induced someone to carry it away for manure." Of this there was naturally no lack in the crowded new quarters of the town. The privies, foul beyond description, were usually in the cellars; it was a common practice to have pigsties under the houses, too, and the pigs roamed the streets once more, as they had not done for centuries in the larger towns. There was even a dire lack of toilets: the "Report on the State of Large Towns and Populous Districts" (1845) states that "in one part of Manchester in 1843-44 the wants of upward 700 inhabitants were supplied by 33 necessaries only—that is, one toilet to every 212 people."

Even at such a low level of design, even with such foul accompaniments, not enough houses were built in many cities; and then far worse conditions prevailed. Cellars were used as dwelling places. In Liverpool, one sixth of the population lived in "underground cellars," and most of the other port cities were not far behind: London and New York were close rivals to Liverpool: even in the nineteen-thirties, there were 20,000 basement dwellings in London medically marked as unfit for human occupation. This dirt and congestion, bad in themselves, brought other pests: the rats that carried bubonic plague, the bedbugs that infested the beds and tormented sleep, the lice that spread typhus, the flies that visited impartially the cellar privy and the infant's food. Moreover the combination of dark rooms and dank walls formed an almost ideal breeding medium for bacteria, especially since the overcrowded rooms afforded the maximum possibilities of transmission through breath and touch.

If the absence of plumbing and municipal sanitation created frightful stenches in these new urban quarters, and if the spread of exposed excrement, together with seepage into local wells, meant a corresponding spread of typhoid, the lack of water was even more sinister. It removed the very possibility of domestic cleanliness or personal hygiene. In the big capital cities, where some of the old municipal traditions still lingered, no adequate provision for water was made in many new areas. In 1809 when London's population was about a million, water was available over the greater part of the city only in the basements of houses. In some quarters, water could be turned on for only three days in a week. And though iron pipes made their appearance in 1746, they were not extensively used until a special act in England in 1817 required that all new mains be built of iron after ten years. . . .

This depression of living quarters was well-nigh universal among the workers in the new industrial towns, once the new industrial regime was fully established. Local conditions sometimes permitted an escape from the extreme of foulness I have been describing: the housing of the millworkers at Manchester, New Hampshire, for example, was of a far superior order; and in the more rural industrial towns of America, particularly in the Middle West, there was at least a little free elbow room and garden space for the workers. But wherever one looks, the improvement was but one of degree: the *type* had definitely changed for the worse.

Charles Dickens

Hard Times

It was a town of red brick, or of brick that would have been red if the smoke and ashes had allowed it; but as matters stood it was a town of unnatural red and black like the painted face of a savage. It was a town of machinery and tall chimneys, out of which interminable serpents of smoke trailed themselves for ever and ever, and never got uncoiled. It had a black canal in it, and a river that ran purple with ill-smelling dye, and vast piles of building full of windows where there was a rattling and a trembling all day long, and where the piston of the steamengine worked monotonously up and down like the head of an elephant in a state of melancholy madness. It contained several large streets all very like one another, and many small streets still more like one another, inhabited by people equally like one another, who all went in and out at the same hours, with the same sound upon the same pavements, to do the same work, and to whom every day was the same as yesterday and tomorrow, and every year the counterpart of the last and the next. . . .

You saw nothing in Coketown but what was severely workful. If the members of a religious persuasion built a chapel there—as the members of eighteen religious persuasions had done—they made it a pious warehouse of red brick, with sometimes (but this is only in highly ornamental examples) a bell in a birdcage on the top of it. The solitary exception was the New Church; a stuccoed edifice with a square steeple over the door, terminating in four short pinnacles like florid wooden legs. All the public inscriptions in the town were painted alike, in severe characters of black and white. The jail might have been the infirmary, the infirmary might have been the jail, the town-hall might have been either, or both, or anything else, for anything that appeared to the contrary in the graces of their construction. Fact, fact, fact, everywhere in the material aspect of the town; fact, fact, fact, everywhere in the immaterial. The M'Choakumchild school was all fact, and the school of design was all fact, and the relations between master and man were all fact, and everything was fact between the lying-in hospital and the cemetery, and what you couldn't state in figures, or show to be purchaseable in the cheapest market and saleable in the dearest, was not, and never should be, world without end, Amen.

A town so sacred to fact, and so triumphant in its assertion, of course got on well? Why no, not quite well. No? Dear me!

No. Coketown did not come out of its own furnaces, in all respects like gold that had stood the fire. First, the perplexing mystery of the place was, Who belonged to the eighteen denominations? Because, whoever did, the labouring people did not. It was very strange to walk through the streets on a Sunday morning, and note how few of *them* the barbarous jangling of bells that was driving the sick and nervous mad, called away from their own quarter, from their own close rooms, from the corners of their own streets, where they lounged listlessly, gazing at all the church and chapel going, as at a thing with which they had no manner of concern. Nor was it merely the stranger who noticed this, because there was a native organization in Coketown itself, whose members were to be heard of in the House of Commons every session, indignantly petitioning for acts of parliament that should make these people religious by main force. Then came the Teetotal Society, who complained that these same people *would* get drunk, and showed in tabular statements that they did get drunk, and proved at tea parties that no inducement, human or Divine (except a medal), would induce them to forego their custom of getting drunk. Then came the chemist and druggist, with other tabular statements, showing that when they didn't get drunk, they took opium. Then came the experienced chaplain of the jail, with more tabular statements, outdoing all the previous tabular statements, and showing that the same people *would* resort to low haunts, hidden from the public eye, where they heard low singing and saw low dancing. . . .

Surely, none of us in our sober senses and acquainted with figures, are to be told at this time of day, that one of the foremost elements in the existence of the Coketown working-people had been for scores of years deliberately set at nought? That there was any Fancy in them demanding to be brought into healthy existence instead of struggling on in convulsions? That exactly in the ratio as they worked long and monotonously, the craving grew within them for some physical relief—

some relaxation, encouraging good humour and good spirits, and giving them a vent
—some recognized holiday, though it were but for an honest dance to a stirring
band of music—some occasional light pie in which even M'Choakumchild had no
finger—which craving must and would be satisfied aright, or must and would inevitably go wrong, until the laws of the Creation were repealed?

George M. Carstairs

Overcrowding
and Human Aggression

When statisticians warn us about the inevitable consequences if recent population
trends are allowed to continue unchecked during the next few generations, our first
concern has naturally been over the basic question of survival: Will the world's
resources suffice to feed all those extra billions? No sooner have we heard the arguments on this than we find ourselves facing the next question: What will be the
quality of the life led by the inhabitants of an overcrowded planet? In particular,
what will be the effects of overcrowding on the manifestations of aggression within
and between societies?

In former centuries, disease and early death exercised so effective a form of
population control that the vast majority of mankind could not indulge in the luxury of aspiring to a high standard of living. Simply to survive into late adulthood,
at the same level of subsistence as one's forefathers, was good fortune enough.
From the time of the earliest prehistoric civilizations to the present day, in almost
every human society, only the privileged elite were in a position to cultivate their
sensibilities and to expand the boundaries of human experience and understanding.
In London, as recently as the beginning of the present century, the very chances of
survival through early infancy were more than twice as high for the children of the
rich as for the children of the poor. Throughout the contemporary world, survival
has become generally attainable, for rich and poor alike; and now, for the first time
in the history of mankind, education, self-awareness, and the aspiration for a meaningful and satisfying life experience are being shared by a majority of people.

Inevitably, once the killing diseases and the threat of starvation have been
averted, people become increasingly aware of, and discontented with, minor forms
of discomfort or unhappiness. One of the striking changes in morbidity in both

From *Violence in America* by Hugh Davis Graham and Ted Robert Gurr, pp. 593-601.
Published by The New American Library, Inc., 1969.

highly developed and in developing countries during recent decades has been the apparent increase in neurosis and psychosomatic disorders. These functional illnesses —which some people prefer to regard as manifestations of "problems of living" rather than of disease—have long been recognized among the privileged classes. Already in 1689, Thomas Sydenham declared that half of his nonfertile patients, that is, one sixth of his total practice, were hysterical; and in 1733, George Cheyne (in his book entitled *The English Disease*) stated that a third of his patients were neurotic.

Both Sydenham and Cheyne were fashionable physicians, most of whose clientele was drawn from the wealthy minority of the English society of their day. Sydenham himself observed that hysteria was commoner among women of the leisured classes than among those who had to toil. It is only in the present day that the working classes have been in a position to enjoy the luxury of being neurotic; but recent surveys, both in Asia and in Manhattan, have shown that the rates for almost every form of mental illness are highest among the socioeconomically underprivileged sections of contemporary societies.

It must be emphasized that the very marked increase in the "visibility" of mental disorders in most countries of the world is partly due to the better control of infections and other serious physical illnesses. Neurosis is a by-product of a raised level of expectation of the quality of life experience when these higher expectations are denied fulfillment. It can, at times, be manifested as what Charles Kingsley called "divine discontent," a spur toward the further enhancement of the standard of living—provided, of course, that steps can be taken to remedy the adverse environmental factors to which the symptoms of neurosis have drawn our attention.

There are, however, many situations in which individuals feel themselves powerless to better their state: conspicuous instances can be found in the socially disorganized slum areas of great cities, especially in periods of very rapid growth such as that experienced by Chicago and Detroit in the early decades of this century, and by such cities as Tokyo, Calcutta, Rio de Janeiro, and other conurbations after the Second World War. Here we are confronted by this vital question: What will be the consequences, for mental health, of a continuing massive increase in human populations? . . .

At first sight, it might seem that much could be learned from observations on species such as lemmings or voles, which are subject to periodic fluctuations of population size. There is still a good deal of controversy among naturalists as to whether these fluctuations are essentially determined by rather gross environmental factors of food supply or infection or whether social interactions also play an important role. Films of lemmings taken during one of their mass migrations have shown that although scarcity of food may be one factor, the movement of the whole population takes on a cumulative momentum as the result of repeated, frenetic interactions, which have been described as showing a hysterical quality.

In recent years the work of ethologists has taught us a great deal about the interaction of innate, biological propensities and learning experiences in many animal species. At a relatively crude level, this can be demonstrated by a modification of the animals' adrenal size and activity. The adrenals play an essential role in an animal's response to stress, whether by fighting or by taking flight. There is a conspicuous difference between the size of the adrenals in wild rats and in rats which have been bred for generations in captivity, the latter having much smaller adrenal glands. When wild rats are caged, and allowed to breed, a diminution in adrenal size becomes apparent in a few generations. In colonies in which there is a great deal of fighting, the mean size of the rats' adrenals increases by up to 30 percent—and this is true both of the aggressors and the victims. Observations in nature have shown marked diminution in adrenal size when rat populations are depleted. For example, the rat population in the sewers of Hamburg at one time became alarmingly large. A vigorous campaign of extermination succeeded literally in decimating their numbers. It was found that the size of the adrenals (in relation to total body size) significantly diminished after the reduction in the rat population. Similar findings were observed when numbers were reduced in an overcrowded herd of deer. . . .

Another instance of the interaction of biological and social factors in the response to stress can be found in observations on the toxity of amphetamine drugs, whose action is similar to that of adrenalin, the secretion of the medulla of the adrenal gland. A relatively small dose of amphetamine will prove fatal to a rat that is confined in a cage with many other rats, whereas a rat that is kept in isolation can survive doses of amphetamine up to four times greater. It is presumed that the effect of the drug is greatly enhanced, in the former situation, by the numerous stressful interactions with the other rats, each of which stimulates the output of more adrenalin until complete exhaustion supervenes. . . .

When animals such as domestic cats, which customarily enjoy quite a wide range of movement, are crowded together in a limited space, there tends to emerge one particularly tyrannical "despot" who holds all the others in fear and also one or more whom Leyhausen terms "pariahs," at the bottom of the status hierarchy. These unfortunate creatures, he observes, are "driven to frenzy and all kinds of neurotic behavior by continuous and pitiless attack by all the others." Although these "pariahs" bear the severest brunt, the whole community of cats held in such close confinement is seen to suffer. These cats "seldom relax, they never look at ease, and there is continuous hissing, growling and even fighting. Play stops altogether, and locomotion and exercise are reduced to a minimum."

This clearly represents a pathological social situation, in which overcrowding and confinement conspire to accentuate disturbing confrontations between individuals. Another observer, studying the behavior of colonies of rats under different degrees of over-population, observed similar changes in their customary interrelationships. Where overcrowding was most marked, the enforced social interactions were seen to interfere with the satisfaction of quite basic biological needs such as feeding, nest building, and the care of their young. Normally mother rats whose nest is disturbed will carry their young, one by one, to a place of safety, but in overcrowded pens this behavior pattern was lost, and the rats' general maternal care became so faulty that in one experiment 80 percent and in another 96 percent of all the young died before reaching maturity. Among the males, some became ascendant over their fellows but others showed a number of disturbances of behavior, of which two patterns were particularly striking: some males appeared to opt out of sexual and social interaction altogether, sulking alone on the periphery of the group, while others became morbidly pensexual, mounting female rats, whether receptive or not, whenever they could do so without being attacked by one of the ascendant males. These hyperactive rats contravened many of the norms of behavior of their group, even becoming cannibal toward the young of their own kind.

It has been maintained by some writers that the human species is unique in its tendency to destroy its own kind; but this is not quite true. Colonies of rats will frequently attack, and even exterminate, single newcomers or groups of "alien" rats that are introduced into their midst. On the other hand, if several rats, previously reared in separate cages, are simultaneously introduced into a strange pen, they will spend several hours exploring the confines of the pen, and each other, without showing aggression; but after a relatively short interval any additional stranger introduced into this newly formed group will be liable to be attacked and killed.

It is, of course, a far cry from the behavior of rats and cats to that of humans; but observations on the behavior of higher primates have a more immediate relevance. Recent studies of apes and monkeys in their natural habitat have greatly modified earlier preconceptions about the frequency of both fighting and sexual behavior. These beliefs were much influenced by observations made by Zuckerman upon apes in zoos, which displayed almost incessant fighting and sexual competition; but this has proved to be only a travesty of their conduct in their natural surroundings. Instead, it is the product of their being confined in overcrowded conditions without the possibility of escape. In the wild state, protective mechanisms operate to control the frequency of both the above types of behavior; but when groups of primates outgrow their territory, the frequency of quarreling and fighting increases.

It is perhaps significant that Leyhausen and Lorenz, the two naturalists who have devoted more attention than almost any others to the disruptive effects of overcrowding, themselves both underwent the painful experience of being closely confined in prisoner-of-war camps for several years. Their personal observations, which have been corroborated by other medical and psychiatric witnesses (e.g., Bettelheim, Cochrane, Gibbens), were that when a group of men was penned up together in close quarters for many months on end, its members tended to become hyperirritable, and to find each other's small mannerisms positively intolerable.

These, too, like the observations on caged cats and rats, were instances of extreme conditions; and yet one must realize that there are many impoverished groups in the world whose conditions of life today are scarcely better. In theory, of course, they can escape from their surroundings; but in practice the "culture of poverty" can induce a sense of despair of ever being able to escape. One is tempted to draw an analogy between the rat that is subjected to a series of physical defeats, or the "pariahs" in an overcrowded colony of cats, and the members of problem families in our city slums who display a seeming inability to make a successful social adaptation. It appears that social institutions and transmitted value systems can create a sense of confinement no less demoralizing than the bars of a cage.

Many years ago, Farris and Dunham drew attention to the ecological concentration of certain forms of mental illness in those parts of a large city where both overcrowding and social 'disorganization—or *anomie* as Durkheim had earlier described it—were most marked. Subsequent research has challenged Dunham's specific contention that schizophrenia is generated by the conditions of life in a socially disorganized community; but many other studies have confirmed his finding that alcoholism, illegitimacy, divorce, delinquency, and numerous other forms of social pathology are most prevalent in such areas.

There remains, however, an interesting contrast in the social correlates of two particular manifestations of social pathology, namely, suicide and attempted suicide—at least, as they are observed in cities of the Western World. Suicide rates are highest in areas where many people live in a state of social isolation, bereft of the support of family, or of any other primary group. On the other hand, studies of attempted suicide have shown that the most important social correlate is overcrowding. Typically, the person who makes a nonfatal suicidal gesture has been harassed beyond endurance by recurrent friction within the domestic group, in cramped and overcrowded premises. Here, too, as in the instance of rats' dose resistance to amphetamine, one can see the mutual reinforcement of multiple factors. A majority of those who attempt suicide are relatively young men and women, who often have had a bad start in life with unstable or absent parent figures. These patients tend to experience great difficulty, in their turn, in forming stable interpersonal relationships: they are often at the same time demanding and inconsiderate toward others, and yet are themselves emotionally immature and dependent. Their deficiencies prompt them to seek out partners from whom they hope to derive support, but all too often the partner whom they select is handicapped in much the same way; so far from meeting each other's dependency needs, these unfortunates only succeed in making each other's state even worse than before. Often, too, they turn to drink or drugs to allay their need for dependence, and this in turn further impoverishes their ability to form rewarding personal relationships.

During recent years many countries have been obliged to take stock of increasing rates of alcoholism, crimes of violence, and attempted suicide. Sociological and social-psychiatric research has shown that there are clusters of disturbances that are found most commonly in overpopulated, underprivileged sectors of large cities; but several interacting factors, in addition to that of overcrowding, are believed to contribute to their appearance. In recent years mass outbreaks of violence have quickened attention to these phenomena. It is disquieting to be reminded that even in countries that have experienced an overall improvement in their standard of living during the last quarter century, an increasing number of people feel alienated from the goals, and the rewards, to which their fellow citizens aspire—and alienated so profoundly that they despair of ever being able to get back into the mainstream of humanity.

Alienation and despair are the product of extreme situations—such as, for example, were realized in the grotesque, doomed societies of the Nazi concentration camps. Many, if not most, of the inmates of such camps found themselves surrendering their customary standards of behavior and their values, becoming completely disoriented by the inhuman conditions under which they were forced to live.

There have been crises in the course of human history when quite large sectors of mankind experienced this sense of alienation from participation in the life of their fellow countrymen. Sometimes after prolonged deprivation their discontents have exploded in outbreaks of revolution, as a result of which a new social order has been created; but at other times leaderless masses of the dispossessed have shown themselves only too ready to become the dupes of mentally unstable yet charismatic demagogues, who promised them a magical deliverance from their miseries. The historian Norman Cohn has shown how often in European history periods of social and economic disruption have resulted in the demoralization of large populations. Cohn has identified a number of social circumstances in which this is liable to occur. Conspicuous among these have been occasions in which long-settled means of production and traditional occupations have been rapidly superseded by new techniques, throwing many individuals out of work; circumstances in which different sectors of a population experience widely contrasting standards of living; and situations where traditional values are weakened, and customary authorities cease to fulfill their protective function. Common to all these circumstances is an all-pervading sense of uncertainty about the future.

George Kennan has epitomized the consequences of such periods of uncertainty with his customary eloquence:

> Whenever the authority of the past is too suddenly and too drastically undermined—whenever the past ceases to be the great and reliable reference book of human problems—whenever, above all; the experience of the father becomes irrelevant to the trials and searchings of the son—there the foundations of man's inner health and stability begin to crumble, insecurity and panic begin to take over, conduct becomes erratic and aggressive.

Just how erratic and aggressive conduct can become in such situations is amply illustrated in Cohn's monograph. He shows that the rootless, uncertain populations who are the victims of too rapid social change tend to regress emotionally, and to clutch at magical solutions for their plight. Nor have leaders been lacking to offer them just such magical solutions, promising a millennium of effortless bliss just around the corner.

A characteristic of these millennial movements has been their tendency to begin on a note of generosity, brotherliness, and willingness to let all share equally in the plenty which is soon to be available. This was the case with the followers of Tanchelm, who inspired a vast following among the poor in Flanders in the early 12th century, and with those of Eudes de l'Etoile, who preached a millennium of universal riches to hordes of peasants in Brittany rendered landless by successive years of famine. Both of these leaders were worshiped as divine during their short heydays.

Two hundred years later, the English "Peasants' Revolt"—fundamentally a rebellion against the feudal relic of villeinage, which restricted laborers' freedom to avail themselves of new forms of employment in trades and manufacturing—found a more down-to-earth leader in John Ball, who contrasted the "natural state of man," born equal and entitled to his fair share of the world's goods, with existing social inequalities. The peroration of one of his addresses went: "Good folk, things cannot go well in England nor ever shall until all things are in common and there is neither villein nor noble, but all of us are of one condition."

The most remarkable of all the European millennial movements was the 2-year reign (1534-36) of the Anabaptist sect in the German town of Münster. Members of this sect proclaimed a universal brotherhood, and held all their possessions in common; but like all their predecessors, they met with vigorous opposition from the established authorities, and this opposition, in every case, provoked counter aggression that was all the more extreme because it was fired with righteous indignation. The benign, ascetic Tanchelm surrounded himself with a ferocious bodyguard; Eudes was executed, threatening to return "on the third day" and wreak vengeance on the oppressors; John Ball soon began to advocate the extermination of all great lords, justices, and priests as a necessary prelude to the Kingdom of the Saints; and the Anabaptists of Münster found themselves tyrannized by a fanatical leader who personally and publicly executed anyone who questioned his "divine" authority.

In parentheses, it is interesting to observe a somewhat similar sequence of events during the [recent] years of student protest. In almost every case, these protests have occurred in vast, rapidly expanded campuses (Berkeley, Columbia, Paris, Rome, Tokyo, etc.) where students felt themselves alienated both personally from their teachers and ideologically from the aims of the university courses. Typically, student protest movements have started with generous, not to say utopian ideals and have taken an ugly turn only when they were confronted with measures of control that were not merely firm, but openly violent. When this happens, the naive slogans of "Flower Power" are soon replaced by cries of "Kill the Pig."

One of Cohn's purposes, in reviewing earlier millennial cults, was to show the similarity between their origins, their magical expectations, and their decline into orgies of "highprincipled" killings and the corresponding sequence of events in Hitler's "thousand-year Reich." Similar outbreaks of unreason have occurred in recent times in less developed societies, typically in one of two social situations. The first occurs when a technologically undeveloped community is suddenly confronted with the material products of the industrialized West. This happened during both World Wars, and led to the outbreak of a series of Cargo Cults that bore a striking resemblance to the earlier European millennial movements, and that like them, began optimistically with promises of magical abundance, encountered the inevitable frustration of the hopes so aroused, and then frequently ended in bitterness and bloodshed. The second situation, familiar to many of the newly liberated colonial countries, is that in which large numbers of the community have developed aspirations for a standard of living long before the economic and political institutions of their country have advanced to the point where these expectations could be fulfilled.

The common theme in all of these examples of the abrogation of common-sense, of contact with reality, and, in the face of frustration, of the unleashing of extremes of violent and destructive behavior, has been the simultaneous arousal of extravagant aspirations together with the shock of realizing that these aspirations are not going to be. The mere juxtaposition of wealth and poverty is not sufficient by itself to excite a spirit of revolt. The stimulus to develop impossible expectations seems to come from a sense of inner insecurity and hopelessness, a total loss of confidence in one's own future. During the postwar era, this has been nowhere more apparant than in the ghettos of the great cities, both in the relatively rich, highly developed societies and in the hungry half of the world. The situation is aggravated when, as a result of uncontrolled population increase, standards of living actually begin to decline at the very time when, by marginal, vicarious participation in a "consumer culture," a people's material aspirations have been raised to new levels.

Today's underprivileged differ from those of previous generations in two respects: their actual poverty is much less severe, and their level of information about their better-off fellows is much greater, thanks to the mass media. As Dr. Sukarno put it, in a much-quoted speech:

> The motion picture industry has provided a window on the world, and the colonized nations have looked through that window and have seen the things of which they have been deprived. It is perhaps not generally realized that a refrigerator can be a revolutionary symbol—to a people who have no refrigerators. A motor car owned by a worker in one country can be a symbol of revolt to a people deprived of the necessities of life.

What he says of undeveloped societies applies with equal force to the impact of movies and television on the aspirations of the less privileged citizens of the technologically advanced countries.

In summary, it seems that overpopulation only aggravates the widespread threat to social stability presented by masses of our population who are basically unsure of their personal future, who have lost confidence in their chance of ever attaining a secure place in their community. It is imperative that we recognize the gravity of this threat because mankind today commands such destructive powers that we cannot afford to risk outbreaks of mass violence; and yet the lesson of history points to the threat of just such disasters. Unless the masses of our city poor can be persuaded that there is a future for them too in the Great Society, their morale is likely to crumble until vast human communities degenerate into the semblance of concentration camp inmates, if not even to that of Zuckerman's pathologically belligerent apes.

Michael K. Drapkin and Thomas L. Ehrich

The Dirty Ohio

PITTSBURGH—The sanitary engineers who assess the water of the Ohio River for drinking purposes use a vivid jargon. Sometimes they describe the water's taste and odor as "cucumber." Sometimes it's "medicinal." And all too often it's "pigpen."

That the Ohio River should sometimes smell like a pigpen discourages conservationists laboring to clean up America's polluted rivers. During the past 20 years, the Ohio has been the target of the broadest cleanup effort ever directed at a U.S. river. . . .

The effect has achieved some success. Most experts agree that the Ohio is indeed cleaner today then at any time since the 1930's. But the amount of filth that still pours into the 981-mile-long Ohio—once known to French explorers as La Belle Riviere—appalls pollution fighters.

BLUISH-BLACK GOO

For example: At Midland, Pa., pipes from a Crucible Steel Corp. titanium plant spew a bright green, poisonous waste fluid into the river. At Steubenville, Ohio, iron oxide from steel company blast furnaces stains the river a reddish brown. Just below Wheeling, W. Va., an Ashland Oil Co. plant pours a bluish-black goo down a bank into the water. Upstream at Aliquippa, Pa., oil discharges from a Jones & Laughlin Steel Corp. plant leave iridescent splotches that flash green and blue as they float lazily away with the current.

Private industry is by no means the only offender. In some spots along the Ohio, a powerful stench of raw sewage wafts across the water, the product of communities that dump their untreated sewage in the river. Three hundred communities on the Ohio and its tributaries have no sewage plants.

Even larger cities that have sewage treatment plants often don't process their sewage adequately. At Pittsburgh, a $100 million plant built in the late 1950's removes lumps of raw sewage, tin cans and other debris from the area's sewer water before it reaches the river. But the 150 million gallons of water that pass through the plant and into the Ohio daily still carry a heavy load of acid, chemicals, oil, grease and brine.

One reason the cleanup of the Ohio is taking so long is that it was an enormous technical task to begin with. Industrialization—and pollution—of the Ohio have been under way for nearly 200 years. The Ohio River Basin, draining an area larger than Germany and the Netherlands combined, is rich with raw materials for the making of iron, steel and chemicals. Three fourths of known U.S. coal reserves underlie the basin, and its forests provide a quarter of the nation's hardwood. The broad, placid river itself provides water, transportation and a means of waste removal for industry and cities. Today the 10-state basin has a population of 24 million, supported by 38,000 industrial plants.

. . .

Over the years, private industry and government alike have tended to regard the Ohio and its tributaries not as something to conserve but as something to use—and a major use is waste disposal. In fact, the main function of most early sewage systems in the basin was to "get the waste into the rivers as fast as possible," says Richard A. Vanderhoof, Cincinnati-based regional director of the Interior Department's Water Pollution Control Agency.

By the end of World War II, the Ohio was almost a dead stream, so laden with pollutants that its waters were unfit for swimming, recreational boating or even many industrial uses. Fish life was practically wiped out.

Leslie A. Chambers

Air Pollution
in Historical Perspective

The quality of the atmosphere, on which existing terrestrial forms of life are dependent, has been recognized as an important variable in the environment only during the past few decades. It can be supposed that smoke and fumes from forest fires, volcanoes, and crude "domestic" heating and cooking arrangements were troublesome or lethal in discrete localities even before our human ancestors became organized into fixed communities; and that the odors of decaying animal and vegetable refuse, attested by existing residues of prehistoric garbage dumps in and near stone age dwellings, were cause for protesting comment in such language as may have been available to the temporary residents.

But it is unlikely that such circumstances can have been regarded as more than incidental to devastating natural cataclysms, or reasons for transfer to another dwelling site, until social evolution reached the husbandry level involving association of family units into more or less fixed communities. Only then could human

From "Classification and Extent of Air Pollution Problems" by Leslie A. Chambers from *Air Pollution*, edited by Arthur C. Stern. Reprinted by permission of Academic Press, Inc.

activities in the aggregate have produced sufficient effluvia to affect an occupied neighborhood. To what extent they did so is entirely conjectural with respect to all of prehistory and can be guessed only by tenuous inference with respect to most of the ancient and medieval periods. The embodiment in folk knowledge of the middle ages, and in prescientific belief, of the concept of "miasmas," or poisonous airs, as etiologic agents of certain diseases, may indicate a deduction from accumulated survival experience related to recognized sources of unwholesome air, but is more likely a mistaken association of "malarias" with the odors of swamps rather than the mosquitos which they supported.

Writers on air pollution occasionally have cited classic references to blackened buildings and monuments as evidence that the smoke nuisance has a reality spanning thousands of years. But the grime of antiquity, while a reasonable expectation, does not suffice to indicate a contemporary recognition of its impact on ancient communities or their members. In fact, accumulated knowledge of domestic heating practices, and of the available primitive metallurgical and other limited industrial processes utilized during the first thirteen or fourteen centuries of the Christian era, leads to the inference that generalized air pollution could not have been an important problem in the villages and towns of the time; cities, in the sense of modern magnitudes, were nonexistent. The frequently cited references to deaths caused by toxic atmospheres, e.g., the suffocation of Pliny and Elder by volcanic fumes as recorded by Tacitus, seem not to be pertinent except in the sense of demonstrating that the human species was then, as it is now, physiologically responsive to anoxia or to poisonous gases.

Throughout the earlier periods of history wood was the prime source of energy; dependence on it undoubtedly slowed the evolution of industrial processes, and eventually limited the per capita availability of heat as depletion of nearby forests proceeded. The discovery of the energy potential of coal, and its gradual displacement of wood, occurred in Europe about the time of Marco Polo's return from his travels through the more technologically advanced civilizations of Asia. But in spite of its abundance in the West, and its retrospectively apparent advantages, the European adaptation to its use which culminated in the Industrial Revolution proceeded slowly and against all the resistance normal to economic readjustments. Coal was an "unnatural" fuel; its sulfurous combustion products confirmed its suspected association with anticlerical forces at a time much too closely related to the ascendancy of strict orthodoxy; and above all, as a matter of record, it caused neighborhood "action committees" to protest against its evident pollution of the atmosphere.

In England, Germany, and elsewhere, various limitations and prohibitions relative to the use, importation, and transport of coal were proclaimed officially, and in isolated instances there is evidence that capital penalities were imposed. Nevertheless the overriding demands for domestic heat and industrial power made these efforts useless and assured their disposal in the limbo of unenforceable law. Coal made possible the Industrial Revolution; and then there was smog.

From the beginning of the fourteenth century to the early part of the twentieth, air pollution by coal smoke and gases occupied the center of the stage almost exclusively, and in many industrialized areas of the world it is still the dominant concern. That it remains a community problem, in spite of repeatedly demonstrated technological capability for its control, would be surprising if public and official hesitance to pay the price were not so characteristic a factor in the evolution of all types of health protective programs. Positive action has seldom been anticipatory; instead it has occurred only after dramatic disasters, or large-scale sensory insults have aroused public clamor based on fear. We build levees only after floods have devastated whole regions; we abate pollution of water supplies only after typhoid epidemics or similarly impressive episodes; and we take necessary action to control air pollutants only after their killing or irritating potentials have been realized on a large scale as in London in 1952 or in Los Angeles around 1945.

In no case is the very early recognition of a public health problem and the failure to take any effective action until it threatened personal survival better illustrated than in the case of air pollution produced by the unrestricted use of coal in Great Britain. During the reign of Edward I (1272-1307) there was recorded a protest, by the nobility, against the use of "sea" coal; and in the succeeding reign of Edward II (1307-1327) a man was put to the torture ostensibly for filling the air with a "pestilential odor" through the use of coal.

Under Richard II (1377-1399) and later under Henry V (1413-1422) England took steps to regulate and restrict the use of coal, apparently because of the smoke and odors produced by its combustion. The earlier action took the form of taxation, while Henry V established a commission to oversee the movement of coal into the City of London.

Other legislation, parliamentary studies, and literary comments appeared sporadically during the following 250 years. In 1661 a notable pamphlet was published by royal command of Charles II. It consisted of an essay entitled "Fumifugium; or the Inconvenience of the Aer and Smoke of London Dissapated; together with Some Remedies Humbly Proposed," written by John Evelyn, one of the founding members of the Royal Society. It is unfortunate that the author's seventeenth century style has attracted more attention in the twentieth century than has the content of his paper. Evelyn clearly recognized the sources, the effects, and the broad aspects of the control problem, to an extent not far surpassed at the present time except for detail and for technological terminology. Thus it is clear, not only that the London of 1661 was plagued by coal smoke, but also that the problem and its content were recognized by at least one of the scientific leaders of the period.

Some evidence exists that methods for abatement of the smoke nuisance were being sought immediately after the appearance of Evelyn's pamphlet, In 1686 a person named Justel presented before the Philosophical Society "An Account of an Engine that Consumes Smoke." The nature of this and other very early control devices is unimportant since the rapid increase in smoke density through the next century and a half indicates that they were, like many more recent procedures, either ineffective or not widely used.

By the beginning of the nineteenth century the smoke nuisance in London and other English cities was of sufficient public concern to prompt the appointment (1819) of a Select Committee of the British Parliament to study and report upon smoke abatement. Immediately available sources do not include the substance of any resulting publication, but the effect of the study is suspected to have been similar to that of dozens of other committee recommendations during the ensuing 147 years. The gradual development of the smoke problem culminated in the action-arousing deaths, in a few days, of 4,000 persons in London in December, 1952.

Records of lethal air pollution concentrations during the nineteenth century are not definitive; in fact, recognition of their occurrence seems to have resulted largely from retrospective examination of vital records and contemporary descriptive notes. In 1873 an episode having the characteristics of the 1952 event occurred in London and more or less severe repetitions have affected metropolitan life at irregular intervals up to the present time.

The term "smog" originated in Great Britain as a popular derivation of "smoke-fog" and appears to have been in common use before World War I. Perhaps the term was suggested by H. A. Des Voeux's 1911 report to the Manchester Conference of the Smoke Abatement League of Great Britain on the smoke-fog deaths which occurred in Glasgow, Scotland in 1909. During two separate periods in the autumn of that year very substantial increases in death rate were attributed to smoke and fog and it was estimated that "1063 deaths were attributable to the noxious conditions."

With few isolated exceptions, the extreme atmospheric concentrations of pollutants produced by coal burning in Britain have not been duplicated elsewhere. Nevertheless, coal-based industrial economies on the continent of Europe and in the United States have caused discomfort, public reaction, and regulatory action. A generation before the dramatic incident which killed 20 and made several hundred ill in the industrial town of Donora, Pennsylvania, in 1948, public protest groups had appeared in several American cities. In some, such as St. Louis, Cincinnati, and more recently in Pittsburgh, popular movements have resulted in substantial elimination of the smoke nuisance, by substitution of less smoky fuels, and by enforced employment of combustion practices designed to eliminate smoke. It has thus been demonstrated that high smoke densities are preventable, although the cost may be large. London and other English cities are handicapped in their current smoke abatement effort by lack of domestic low-volatility coal supplies, almost complete dependence on imports for other fossil fuels, and a centuries-old pattern of household heating, the physical characteristics of which can be changed only gradually and at a very high price.

No rigorous identification of the constituents of coal smoke responsible for the respiratory illnesses with which it has been associated has been produced, although the effects have been generally attributed to sulfur dioxide and trioxide. Recently the probability of a role of tar, soot, and ash particles in the total irritative effect has been the inspiration for several investigations. But the information available to us on the relationship of coal smoke to human health has been insufficient to explain fully the death and discomfort it has caused.

Smoke and gases from the burning of coal have been the chief atmospheric pollutants in all parts of the industrialized world for more than 400 years. In spite of the recent rapid shift to petroleum and natural gas, coal smoke still is a major contributor to poor air quality in most urbanized areas.

Robert Rienow and Leona Train Rienow

A Matter of Life and Breath

A recent scientific analysis of New York City's atmosphere concluded that a New Yorker on the street took into his lungs the equivalent in toxic materials of 38 cigarettes a day. Suddenly all the scientific jargon, official warnings, reams of statistics—the overwhelming avalanche of damning facts concerning America's air pollution—took focus. Here was a reduction of the tons of soot, sulphides, monoxide, hydrocarbons, etc., into simple, understandable, personal terms.

These figures are of vital interest to two thirds of the population, which is the percentage of Americans who already live in 212 standard metropolitan areas having only 9 percent of the nation's land area but 99 percent of its pollution. Some cities outdo Manhattan and on days of cloud and atmospheric inversion actually kill off small segments of their excess population (involuntarily, of course).

Smog production seems to be a cooperative effort among our great cities. "A great deal of the smoke and dirty air in New York City comes each morning from the industrial areas of New Jersey," accused former Mayor Wagner as, smiling apologetically, he testified at an October, 1964, hearing on air pollution. Then his innate fairness forced him to add: "We return the compliment each afternoon, depending on the prevailing winds, or we pass some of our smoke and gases on to our Long Island or Connecticut neighbors."

But, definitely, New York was getting the worst of everything. It is "the terminus of a 3,000-mile-long sewer of atmospheric filth starting as far away as California and growing like a dirty snowball all the way." New Jersey's champion, Chairman William Bradley of the state's pollution control commission, felt that it was New Jersey who was really behind the eight ball or, rather, dirty snowball. "We feel incapable of coping," he sighed dramatically.

What, actually, is it we are talking about when we rant about air pollution? What it is varies from city to city and from industrial complex to industrial complex.

Excerpts from *Moment in the Sun* bu Robert Rienow and Leona Train Rienow, pp. 111-113, 115-116, 122. Copyright © 1967 by Robert Rienow and Leona Train Rienow. Reprinted by permission of The Dial Press and Paul R. Reynolds, Inc.

There is a conglomeration of particles—bits of metal, the metallic oxides, tar, stone, carbon, and ash, the aerosols, mists of oils, and all manner of soot.

Strangely enough, Anchorage, Alaska, in the clear and pristine North, excels in this air filth, with Charleston, West Virginia, East Chicago, Phoenix, and Los Angeles treading eagerly on its heels. The electrostatic precipitator in a factory chimney or the use of a whirling water bath for smoke emissions can remove many of these solids, but such devices cost money, and money (and the treasuring thereof) is still our number one consideration.

Much more serious than filthy particles is the sulphur dioxide that comes from the combustion of all heavy fuel oils, coal, and coke. We have visual evidence that this substance eats away brick, stone, and metal bridges, but we have not taken time off to discover what it does to the human lung. A derivative, sulphur trioxide, is the common sulphuric acid, which we know eats into the lungs, eyes, and skin, but again research as to how to extirpate it from the air we breathe does not add appreciably to the GNP.

Technology's contribution to the air we breathe includes—in addition to the particulates, aerosols, and sulphur oxides—a whole legion of grisly gases, among them, carbon dioxide, carbon monoxide, hydrofluoric acid, hydrochloric acid, ammonia, organic solvents, aromatic benzypyrene, deadly ozone, and perhaps another 500 or more lethal emissions (some day we shall have discovered thousands). A few years ago the oil refineries and factories were assigned most of the blame for city smog; later, incinerators took the abuse; at length it was demonstrated beyond a doubt that from 60 to 85 percent of most city smog is caused by man's best friend, the effusive automobile.

Such smog, strangely enough, has lately been discovered to be the result of the action of sunlight on the incompletely combusted automobile exhaust gases, mainly carbon monoxide, the hydrocarbons, and nitrogen oxides. An unbelievably complex and varied "mishmash" of photochemical reactions takes place all day long from dawn to dark. Out of this witches' cauldron, whose catalyst is the sunshine, emerges a whole army of killing compounds: olefins (synergetic hydrocarbons "hungry to react to something"), ketene, peroxyacetylnitrate, sulphuric acid, aldehydes, and, probably most vicious of all, ozone. The automobile is a versatile chemical factory that can produce almost anything you might wish to dial. Of all these perverse and malicious agents, man knows as yet almost nothing about what they do to humans over a period of time. . . .

A cartoon of a few years ago presenting the inside of a U.S. weather station of the future depicted the weatherman making the following report: "Our latest analysis of the stratosphere, Dr. Figby! . . . 21 percent hydrogen, 7 percent oxygen . . . and 72 percent automobile exhaust fumes!" By 1985 this cartoon will no longer amuse. Predicts sanitation expert A. C. Stern of the Taft Sanitary Engineering Center, Cincinnati: By 1985 the U.S. Weather Bureau will be issuing daily air pollution reports as well as weather forecasts. People will be "more interested in whether it will be safe to breathe than whether it will be rainy or sunny." Our only comment here is that his prediction is for ten—probably fifteen—years too late. . . .

There are, in all, from 8,000 to 10,000 tons of gases, vapors, and solids being thrown into a large city's air every day—a generous two thirds of it from the automobile—to saturate the lungs of roughly two thirds of the nation's population. Years ago former Surgeon General Leroy T. Burney declared categorically that there is a "definite association between community air pollution and high mortality rates," a fact that is today universally accepted.

While cars get faster and longer, lives get slower and shorter. While Chrysler competes with Buick for the getaway, cancer competes with emphysema for the layaway. This generation is indeed going to have to choose between humans and the automobile. Perhaps most families have too many of both.

5

Toward an Ethic of Environment

In a sense we have become victims of our own intelligence. Our industrial mentality and capacity applied to our environment has strengthened the assumption that somehow we are not subject to the laws of nature that bind other living things. Humans alone have developed technology and humans alone have learned to live so abundantly. We have also developed the attitude that there is nothing we cannot do. We have no doubt that we will progress and cannot believe we are not invincible. Superior to our surroundings, we alone try to violate the laws of nature with impunity.

In the first selection that follows, Ian L. McHarg demolishes the immoderate notions of human superiority. He makes a compelling case for the interdependence of humanity and nature. Humanity is an aspect of nature, occupies a niche in the natural order of things, and disrupts that order only with grave risks to human well-being. McHarg indicates that the traditional belief that human beings are unique, living above and beyond the rest of creation is no more than a self-delusion created by humanity's truly unique reason and imagination. Genuine rationality, however, consists in our appreciating our real role in nature.

The unrestrained egotism of the belief in our singular role and the hubristic claim of our inherent right to bend nature to our will inspired our unthinking devotion to Progress, at whose alter we have worshiped for centuries. Only now are we beginning to recognize that progress is not simply technology's race forward into ever-improved tomorrows; it is also a process whose by-products include environmental destruction so violent, widespread, and even irreversible that our continued existence is threatened.

It has become obvious that we have inflicted such immense insults upon the environment in the name of progress that the industrial-technological wonder we have created has become a monster that could very well destroy us. As our power over the environment has gotten out of control, we have come to doubt the efficacy of progress. W. R. Inge suggests that progress has been accepted with such blind, stupid faith that it has become a disease of modern life. He asserts that we have made no progress at all where it really counts—in changing human nature. And he establishes that progress has not really meant success. Inge's doubts about the utility of progress reflect Ralph Waldo Emerson's grim warning that we will die of civilization.

Joseph Wood Krutch shares this distrust of progress. He maintains that humans must abandon their traditional role as exploiters of nature and learn to live in sympathetic harmony with the environment. He would agree with Ogden Nash that "progress may have been alright once, but it went on too long." Krutch calls upon us to stop applying economic values to the environment and to begin judging all life by an ethical standard. Our attitude toward nature must become a matter of right and wrong. He echoes the cogent ideas of conservation pioneer Aldo Leopold, who advocated adherence to a "land ethic": recognition that people belong to the land as much as the land belongs to people and that the two must coexist through intimate interaction. In a lifetime of nature writing, Krutch celebrated the aesthetic value of environments still free of human domination and despoliation. But he also recognized the fact that human destiny is inescapably a part of natural history.

Krutch is asking for nothing less than that humanity change its historic attitude of mastery over the environment to one of unity with all creation. Perhaps, if we are to overcome the crisis of environmental decay, Krutch's love of nature and Leopold's land ethic must become a credo for us all—worship beauty in nature and not in progress.

Over many generations the human species has proven itself to be highly adaptable to life's changing conditions. From their very beginnings human beings have adjusted their life style to fit novel circumstances. In recent generations they even have proven themselves capable of living in the offensive conditions of overcrowding and a decaying environment. Adaptability is the foundation for the survival of any group of living things. Human survival potential has been infinitely extended by the power to create culture and, through technology, to devise cultural artifacts that both enhance natural adaptability and permit modification of the environment. But some would maintain that survival is not enough.

René Dubos is one who holds that we must have more than life; we must have quality life. He finds that modern humanity is tied closely to its Paleolithic ancestors by the innate desire to enjoy life in close interplay with nature, but that we are forced by modern surroundings to compromise this desire in the pursuit of what in fact is an "inhuman" existence. He maintains that much of "humanness" has already been sacrificed in our effort to adapt to crowding, filth, and pollution—the circumstances of life in a technologically progressive civilization. Like Joseph Wood Krutch, Dubos argues for a quality life for people in concert with a quality environment.

The ecological crisis is the result of our ability to alter our natural environment. The confrontation is not simply civilization against nature. Human nature has made civilization an aspect of the human condition. But if that condition is to be tolerable, an accommodation must be made between our creative and destructive powers and the capacity of this planet to abide human enterprise. Ironically, human creativity has provided remarkable adaptability and facilitated human survival. Now that creativity is itself proving maladaptive and its momentum must be overcome if both humanity and nature are to be served. Krutch and Dubos point the way toward an accord between humans and nature. They show that we must apply ethical standards to all human conduct, must recognize the real value of the environment, and must create an improved existence within the framework of nature. Failing this, humanity risks a future that is increasingly unnatural, dangerous, ugly, and inhuman.

We may be able to survive in a world where most of the works of nature have been destroyed and replaced by our own creations. But existence will be informed by the needs and character of artificial mechanisms. The disappearance of all living things save human beings will extinguish the value and meaning of life itself. In such a world both nature and humanity will have become superfluous.

Ian L. McHarg

Our Role in Nature

The nature and scale of this enquiry can be simply introduced through an image conceived by Loren Eiseley. Man, far out in space, looks back to the distant earth, a celestial orb, blue-green oceans, green of verdant land, a celestial fruit. Examination discloses blemishes on the fruit, dispersed circles from which extend dynamic tentacles. The man concludes that these cankers are the works of man and asks, "Is man but a planetary disease?"

There are at least two conceptions within this image. Perhaps the most important is the view of a unity of life covering the earth, land and oceans, interacting as a single superorganism, the biosphere. A direct analogy can be found in man, composed of billion upon billion of cells but all of these operating as a single organism. From this the full relevance of the second conception emerges, the possibility that man is but a dispersed disease in the world-life body.

The conception of all life interacting as a single superorganism is as novel as is the conception of man as a planetary disease. The suggestion of man the destroyer, or rather brain the destroyer, is salutary to society which has traditionally abstracted brain from body, man from nature, and vaunted the rational process. This, too, is a recent view. Yet the problems are only of yesterday. Pre-atomic man was an inconsequential geological, biological, and ecological force; his major power was the threat of power. Now, in an instant, post-atomic man is the agent of evolutionary regression, a species now empowered to destroy all life.

In the history of human development, man has long been puny in the face of overwhelmingly powerful nature. His religions, philosophies, ethics and acts have tended to reflect a slave mentality, alternately submissive or arrogant toward nature. Judaism, Christianity, Humanism tend to assert outrageously the separateness and dominance of man over nature, while animism and nature worship tend to assert total submission to an arbitrary nature. These attitudes are not urgent when human societies lack the power to make any serious impact on environment. These same attitudes become of first importance when man holds the power to cause evolutionary regressions of unimaginable effect or even to destroy all life.

Modern man is confronted with the awful problem of comprehending the role of man in nature. He must immediately find a *modus vivendi*, he must seek beyond for his role in nature, a role of unlimited potential yet governed by laws which he shares with all physical and organic systems. The primacy of man today is more based upon his power to destroy than to create. He is like an aboriginal,

Excerpted from Chapter 5, "Man and Environment" by Ian L. McHarg in *The Urban Condition* edited by Leonard J. Duhl; ©1963 by Basic Books, Inc., Publishers, New York. Reprinted by permission.

confronted with the necessity of operating a vast and complex machine, whose
only tool is a hammer. Can modern man aspire to the role of agent in creation,
creative participant in a total, unitary, evolving environment? If the pre-atomic past
is dominated by the refinement of concern for man's acts towards man, the inaugu-
ration of the atomic age increases the dimension of this ancient concern and now
adds the new and urgent necessity of understanding and resolving the interdependence of man and nature. . . .

NATURAL SCIENCE AND NATURALISM

It might be productive to examine the natural scientist's view of the evolution of
nature and certain aspects of this order. The astronomer gives us some idea of immensity of scale, a hundred billion galaxies receding from us at the speed of light.
Of these hundred billion galaxies is one which is our own, the Milky Way. Eccentric
within the immensity of the Milky Way, the inconspicuous solar system exists.
Within the immensity of the solar system, revolves the minute planet, Earth. The
astronomer and geologist together give us some sense of the process during which
the whirling, burning gases increased in density, coalesced with cooling, condensed,
gave off steam, and finally produced a glassy sphere, the Earth. This sphere with
land and oceans had an atmosphere with abundant carbon dioxide, with abundant
methane, and little or no free oxygen. A glassy sphere with great climatic ranges in
temperature, diurnal and seasonal, comparable to an alternation between Arctic
and Equatorial conditions. From the biologist we learn of the origins of life. The
first great miracle of life was this plant-animal in the sea; the emergence of life on
land, the succession of fungi, mosses, liverworts, ferns. The miracle beyond life is
photosynthesis, the power by which plants, absorbing carbon dioxide, give out
oxygen and use the sun's energy to transform light into substance. The substance
becomes the source of food and fuel for all other forms of life. There seems to be
good reason to believe that the Earth's atmosphere, with abundant oxygen, is a
product of the great evolutionary succession of plants. On them we depend for all
food and fossil fuels. From the botanist we learn of the slow colonization of the
Earth's surface by plants, the degree to which the surface of the Earth was stabi-
lized, and, even more significantly, how plants modified the climatic extremes to
support the amphibian, reptilian, and subsequent mammalian evolutionary
sequence.

    The transcendental view of man's relation to nature implicit in Western phi-
losophies is dependent upon the presumption that man does in fact exist outside
of nature, that he is not dependent upon it. In contemporary urban society the
sense of absolute dependence and interdependence is not apparent, and it is an
extraordinary experience to see a reasonably intelligent man become aware of the
fact that his survival is dependent upon natural processes, not the least of which are
based upon the continued existence of plants. This relationship can be demonstrated by experiment with three major characters: light, man, and algae. The the-
ater is a cylinder in which is a man, a certain quantity of algae, a given quantity of

water, a given quantity of air, and a single input, a source of light corresponding to sunlight (in this case a fluorescent tube). The man breathes the air, utilizes the oxygen, and exhales carbon dioxide. The algae utilize the carbon dioxide and exhale oxygen. There is a closed cycle of carbon dioxide and oxygen. The man consumes water, passes the water, the algae consume the water, the water is transpired, collected, and the man consumes the water. There is a closed water cycle. The man eats the algae, the man passes excrement, the algae consume the excrement, the man consumes the algae. There is a closed cycle of food. The only input is light. In this particular experiment the algae is as dependent upon the man as the man is upon the algae. In nature this is obviously not true. For some two billion years nature did exist without man. There can, however, be absolutely no doubt about the indispensability of the algae or plant photosynthesis to the man. It is the single agent able to utilize radiant energy from the sun and make it available as products to support life. This experiment very clearly shows the absolute dependence of man on nature.

Man has claimed to be unique. Social anthropologists have supported this claim on the ground that he alone has the gift of communication, and again that he alone has values. It might be worthwhile considering this viewpoint. A very famous biologist, Dr. David Goddard, said that a single human sperm, weighing one billionth of a gram, contains more information coded into its microscopic size than all of the information contained in all of the libraries of all men in all time. This same statement can be made for the seed of other animals or plants. This is a system of communication which is not rational, but which is extraordinarily delicate, elegant, and powerful, and which is capable of transmitting unimaginable quantities of information in microscopic volume.

This system of communication has enabled all species to survive the evolutionary time span. All forms of extant life share this system of communication; man's participation in it is in no sense exceptional.

Man also claims a uniqueness for himself on the grounds that he alone, of all of the animals, has values from which cultural objectives are derived. It would appear that the same *genetic* system of communication also contains a *value system.* Were this not so, those systems of organic life which do persist today would not have persisted; the genetic information transmitted is the information essential for survival. That information insures the persistence of the organism within its own ecological community. The genetic value system also contains the essential mutation; that imperfection essential for evolution and survival. This system of communication is elegant, beautiful, and powerful, capable of sifting enormous numbers of conflicting choices. Man participates in and shares this system, but his participation is in no sense exceptional.

Yet another aspect of man's assumption that he is independent of natural processes is the anthropomorphic attitude which implies a finite man who is born, grows, and dies, but who during his life is made of the same unchanging stuff—himself. Not so. If we simply measure that which man ingests, and rejects, we begin to doubt this premise. Hair, nails, skin, and chemical constituents are replaced regularly. He replaces several billion cells daily. The essential stuff of man is changed very regularly indeed. In a much more fundamental way, however, man is a creature of environment. We have learned that he is absolutely dependent upon stimuli —light, shadow, color, sound, texture, gravity; and upon his sense of smell, taste, touch, vision, and hearing. These constantly changing environmental conditions are his references. Without them there would be hallucination, hysteria, perhaps mental disintegration, certainly loss of reality.

THE ECOLOGICAL VIEW

It remains for the biologist and ecologist to point out the interdependence which characterizes all relationships, organic and inorganic, in nature. It is the ecologist who points out that an ecological community is only able to survive as a result of interdependent activity between all of the species which constitute the community. To the basic environment (geology, climate), is added an extraordinary complexity of inert materials, their reactions, and the interaction of the organic members of the community with climate, inert materials, and other organisms. The characteristic of life is interdependence of all of the elements of the community upon each other. Each one of these is a source of stimulus; each performs work; each is part of a pattern, a system, a working cycle; each one is to some lesser or greater degree a participant and contributor in a thermodynamic system. This interdependence common to nature—common to all systems—is in my own view the final refutation of man's assumption of independence. It appears impossible to seperate man from this system. It would appear that there is a system, the order of which we partly observe. Where we observe it, we see interdependence, not independence, as a key. This interdependence is in absolute opposition to Western man's presumption of transcendence, his presumption of independence, and, of course, his presumption of superiority, dominion, and license to subdue the earth.

A tirade on the theme of dependence is necessary only to a society which views man as independent. Truly there is in nature no independence. Energy is the basis for all life; further, no organism has, does, or will live without an environment. All systems are depletive. There can be no enduring system occupied by a single organism. The minimum, in a laboratory experiment, requires the presence of at least two complementary organisms. These conceptions of independence and anthropocentrism are baseless.

The view of organisms and environment widely held by natural scientists is that of interdependence—symbiosis. Dr. Paul Sears of Yale University has written:

> Any species survives by virtue of its niche, the opportunity afforded it by environment. But in occupying this niche, it also assumes a role in relation to its surroundings. For further survival it is necessary that its role at least be not a disruptive one. Thus, one generally finds in nature that each component of a highly organized community serves a constructive, or, at any rate, a stabilizing role. The habitat furnishes the niche, and if any species breaks up the

habitat, the niche goes with it. . . . That is, to persist they [ecological communities] must be able to utilize radiant energy not merely to perform work, but to maintain the working system in reasonably good order. This requires the presence of organisms adjusted to the habitat and to each other, so organized as to make the fullest use of the influent radiation and to conserve for use and re-use the materials which the system requires. The degree to which a living community meets these conditions is therefore a test of its efficiency and stability.

Man, too, must meet this test. Dr. Sears states:

Man is clearly the beneficiary of a very special environment which has been a great while in the making. This environment is more than a mere inert stockroom. It is an active system, a pattern and a process as well. Its value can be threatened by disruption no less than by depletion.

The natural scientist states that no species can exist without an environment, no species can exist in an environment of its exclusive creation, no species can survive, save as a non-disruptive member of an ecological community. Every member must adjust to other members of the community and to the environment in order to survive. Man is not excluded from this test.

Man must learn this prime ecological lesson of interdependence. He must see himself linked as a living organism to all living and all preceding life. This sense may impel him to understand his interdependence with the micro-organisms of the soil, the diatoms in the sea, the whooping crane, the grizzly bear, sand, rocks, grass, trees, sun, rain, moon, and stars. When man learns this he will have learned that when he destroys he also destroys himself; that when he creates, he also adds to himself. When man learns the single lesson of interdependence he may be enabled to create by natural process an environment appropriate for survival. This is a fundamental precondition for the emergence of man's role as a constructive and creative agent in the evolutionary process. Yet this view of interdependence as a basis for survival, this view of man as a participant species in an ecological community and environment, is quite contrary to the Western view.

. . . The creation of a physical environment by organisms, as individuals and as communities, is not exclusively a human skill; it is shared with the bee, the coral, and the chambered nautilus, which take inert materials and dispose them to create a physical environment, complementary to—indeed, indispensable to—the organism.

When man abandoned instinct for rational thought, he abandoned the powers that permitted him to emulate such organisms; if rationality alone sufficed, man should at least be able to equal these humble organisms. But thereby hangs a parable:

The nuclear cataclysm is over. The earth is covered with gray dust. In the vast silence no life exists, save for a little colony of algae hidden deep in a leaden cleft long innured to radiation. The algae perceive their isolation; they reflect upon the strivings of all life, so recently ended, and on the strenuous task of evolution to be begun anew. Out of their reflection could emerge a firm conclusion: "Next time, no brains."

William Ralph Inge

The Idea of Progress

The belief in Progress, not as an ideal but as an indisputable fact, not as a task for humanity but as a law of Nature, has been the working faith of the West for about [two hundred] years. . . .

In the seventeenth century a doctrine of progress was already in the air, and a long literary battle was waged between the Ancients and the Moderns. But it was only in the eighteenth century that Western Europe began to dream of an approaching millennium without miracle, to be gradually ushered in under the auspices of a faculty which was called Reason. Unlike some of their successors, these optimists believed that perfection was to be attained by the self-determination of the human will; they were not fatalists. In France, the chief home of this heady doctrine, the psychical temperature soon began to rise under its influence, till it culminated in the delirium of the Terror. The Goddess of Reason hardly survived Robespierre and his guillotine; but the belief in progress, which might otherwise have subsided when the French resumed their traditional pursuits—*rem militarem et argute loqui*—was reinforced by the industrial revolution, which was to run a very different course from that indicated by the theatrical disturbances at Paris between 1789 and 1794, the importance of which has perhaps been exaggerated. In England above all, the home of the new industry, progress was regarded (in the words which Mr. Mallock puts into the mouth of a nineteenth-century scientist) as that kind of improvement which can be measured by statistics. This was quite seriously the view of the last century generally, and there has never been, nor will there ever be again, such an opportunity for gloating over this kind of improvement. The mechanical inventions of Watt, Arkwright, Crompton, Stephenson, and others led to an unparalleled increase of population. Exports and imports also progressed, in a favorite phrase of the time, by leaps and bounds. Those who, like Malthus, sounded a note of warning, showing that population increases, unlike the supply of food, by geometrical progression, were answered that compound interest follows the same admirable law.

From "The Idea of Progress" from *Outspoken Essays* by William Ralph Inge. Reprinted by permission of Greenwood Press, Inc. and Longman Group Limited.

It was obvious to many of our grandparents that a nation which travels sixty miles an hour must be five times as civilized as one which travels only twelve. . . .

If we turn to history for a confirmation of the Spencerian doctrine, we find on the contrary, that civilization is a disease which is almost invariably fatal, unless its course is checked in time. The Hindus and Chinese, after advancing to a certain point, were content to mark time; and they survive. But the Greeks and Romans are gone; and aristocracies everywhere die out. Do we not see today the complex organization of the ecclesiastic and college don succumbing before the simple squeezing and sucking apparatus of the profiteer and trade-unionist? If so-called civilized nations show any protracted vitality, it is because they are only civilized at the top. Ancient civilizations were destroyed by imported barbarians; we breed our own.

It is also an unproved assumption that the domination of the planet by our own species is a desirable thing, which must give satisfaction to its Creator. We have devastated the loveliness of the world; we have exterminated several species more beautiful and less vicious than ourselves; we have enslaved the rest of the animal creation, and have treated our distant cousins in fur and feathers so badly that beyond doubt, if they were able to formulate a religion, they would depict the Devil in human form. If it is progress to turn the fields and woods of Essex into East and West Ham, we may be thankful that progress is a sporadic and transient phenomenon in history. . . .

There has been no physical progress in our species for many thousands of years. The Cro-Magnon race, which lived perhaps twenty thousand years ago, was at least equal to any modern people in size and strength; the ancient Greeks were, I suppose, handsomer and better formed than we are; and some unprogressive races, such as the Zulus, Samoans, and Tahitians, are envied by Europeans for either strength or beauty. Although it seems not to be true that the sight and hearing of civilized peoples are inferior to those of savages, we have certainly lost our natural weapons, which from one point of view is a mark of degeneracy, Mentally, we are now told that the men of the Old Stone Age, ugly as most of them must have been, had as large brains as ours; and he would be a bold man who should claim that we are intellectually equal to the Athenians or superior to the Romans. The question of moral improvement is much more difficult. Until the Great War few would have disputed that civilized man had become much more humane, much more sensitive to the sufferings of others, and so more just, more self-controlled, and less brutal in his pleasures and in his resentments. The habitual honesty of the Western European might also have been contrasted with the rascality of inferior races in the past and present. It was often forgotten that, if progress means the improvement of human nature itself, the question to be asked is whether the modern civilized man behaves better in the same circumstances than his ancestor would have done. Absence of temptation may produce an appearance of improvement; but this is hardly what we mean by progress, and there is an old saying that the Devil has a clever trick of pretending to be dead. It seems to me very doubtful whether when we are exposed to the same temptations we are more humane or more sympathetic or juster or less brutal than the ancients. . . .

We have, then, been driven to the conclusion that neither science nor history gives us any warrant for believing that humanity has advanced, except by accumulating knowledge and experience and the instruments of living. The value of these accumulations is not beyond dispute. Attacks upon civilization have been frequent, from Crates, Pherecrates, Antisthenes, and Lucretius in antiquity to Rousseau, Walt Whitman, Thoreau, Ruskin, Morris, and Edward Carpenter in modern times. I cannot myself agree with these extremists. I believe that the accumulated experience of mankind, and his wonderful discoveries, are of great value. I only point out that they do not constitute real progress in human nature itself, and that in the absence of any real progress these gains are external, precarious, and liable to be turned to our own destruction.

Joseph Wood Krutch

The Conservation Ethic

Moralists often blame races and nations because they have never learned how to live and let live. In our time we seem to have been increasingly aware how persistently and brutally groups of men undertake to eliminate one another. But it is not only the members of his own kind that man seems to want to push off the earth. When he moves in, nearly everything else suffers from his intrusion—sometimes because he wants the space they occupy and the food they eat, but often simply because when he sees a creature not of his kind or a man not of his race his first impulse is "kill it."

Hence it is that even in the desert, where space is cheaper than in most places, the wildlife grows scarcer and more secretive as the human population grows. The coyote howls farther and farther off. The deer seek closer and closer cover. To almost everything except man the smell of humanity is the most repulsive of all odors, the sight of man the most terrifying of all sights. Biologists call some animals "cryptozoic," that is to say "leading hidden lives." But as the human population increases most animals develop, as the deer has been developing, cryptozoic habits. Even now there are more of them around than we realize. They see us when we do not see them—because they have seen us first. Albert Schweitzer remarks somewhere that we owe kindness even to an insect when we can afford to show it, just because we ought to do something to make up for all the cruelties, necessary

From "Conservation is Not Enough" from *The Best Nature Writing of Joseph Wood Krutch* by Joseph Wood Krutch, pp. 370-375, 378-381, 382-384. Reprinted by permission of William Morrow and Company, Inc. Copyright © 1955 by Joseph Wood Krutch.

as well as unnecessary, which we have inflicted upon almost the whole of animate creation.

Probably not one man in ten is capable of understanding such moral and aesthetic considerations, much less of permitting his conduct to be guided by them. But perhaps twice as many, though still far from a majority, are beginning to realize that the reckless laying waste of the earth has practical consequences. They are at least beginning to hear about "conservation," though they are not even dimly aware of any connection between it and a large morality and are very unlikely to suppose that "conservation" does or could mean anything more than looking after their own welfare.

Hardly more than two generations ago Americans first woke up to the fact that their land was not inexhaustible. Every year since then more and more has been said, and at least a little more has been done about "conserving resources," about "rational use," and about such reconstruction as seemed possible. Scientists have studied the problem, public works have been undertaken, laws passed. Yet everybody knows that the using up still goes on, perhaps not so fast nor so recklessly as once it did, but unmistakably nevertheless. And there is nowhere that it goes on more nakedly, more persistently, or with a fuller realization of what is happening than in the desert regions where the margin to be used up is narrower.

First, more and more cattle were set to grazing and overgrazing the land from which the scanty rainfall now ran off even more rapidly than before. More outrageously still, large areas of desert shrub were rooted up to make way for cotton and other crops watered by wells tapping underground pools of water which are demonstrably shrinking fast. These pools represent years of accumulation not now being replenished and are exhaustible exactly as an oil well is exhaustible. Everyone knows that they will give out before long, very soon, in fact, if the number of wells continues to increase as it has been increasing. Soon dust bowls will be where was once a sparse but healthy desert, and man, having uprooted, slaughtered, or driven away everything which lived healthily and normally there, will himself either abandon the country or die. There are places where the creosote bush is a more useful plant than cotton.

To the question why men will do or are permitted to do such things there are many answers. Some speak of population pressures, some more brutally of unconquerable human greed. Some despair; some hope that more education and more public works will, in the long run, prove effective. But is there, perhaps, something more, something different, which is indispensable? Is there some missing link in the chain of education, law, and public works? Is there not something lacking without which none of these is sufficient?

After a lifetime spent in forestry, wildlife management, and conservation of one kind or another, after such a lifetime during which he nevertheless saw his country slip two steps backward for every one it took forward, the late Aldo Leopold pondered the question and came up with an unusual answer which many people would dismiss as "sentimental" and be surprised to hear from a "practical" scientific man. He published his article orginally in the *Journal of Forestry* and it was reprinted in the posthumous volume, *A Sand County Almanac,* where it was given the seemingly neutral but actually very significant title "The Land Ethic."

This is a subtle and original essay full of ideas never so clearly expressed before and seminal in the sense that each might easily grow into a separate treatise. Yet the conclusion reached can be simply stated. Something *is* lacking and because of that lack education, law, and public works fail to accomplish what they hope to accomplish. Without that something, the high-minded impulse to educate, to legislate, and to manage becomes as sounding brass and tinkling cymbals. And the thing which is missing is love, some feeling for, as well as some understanding of, the inclusive community of rocks and soils, plants and animals, of which we are a part.

It is not, to put Mr. Leopold's thoughts in different words, enough to be enlightenedly selfish in our dealings with the land. That means, of course, that it is not enough for the farmer to want to get the most out of his farm and the lumberer to get the most out of his forest without considering agriculture and wood production as a whole both now and in the future. But it also means more than that. In the first place, enlightened selfishness cannot be enough because enlightened selfishness cannot possibly be extended to include remote posterity. It may include the children, perhaps, and grandchildren, possibly, but it cannot be extended much beyond that because the very idea of "self" cannot be stretched much further. Some purely ethical considerations must operate, if anything does. Yet even that is not all. The wisest, the most enlightened, the most remotely long-seeing exploitation of resources is not enough, for the simple reason that the whole concept of exploitation is so false and so limited that in the end it will defeat itself and the earth will have been plundered no matter how scientifically and farseeingly the plundering has been done.

To live healthily and successfully on the land we must also live with it. We must be part not only of the human community, but of the whole community; we must acknowledge some sort of oneness not only with our neighbors, our countrymen, and our civilization, but also some respect for the natural as well as for the man-made community. Ours is not only "one world" in the sense usually implied by that term. It is also "one earth." Without some acknowledgement of that fact, men can no more live successfully than they can if they refuse to admit the political and economic interdependency of the various sections of the civilized world. It is not a sentimental but a grimly literal fact that unless we share this terrestrial globe with creatures other than ourselves, we shall not be able to live on it for long.

You may, if you like, think of this as a moral law. But if you are skeptical about moral laws, you cannot escape the fact that it has its factual, scientific aspect. Every day the science of ecology is making clearer the factual aspect as it demonstrates those more and more remote interdependencies which, no matter how remote they are, are crucial even for us.

Before even the most obvious aspects of the balance of nature had been recognized, a greedy, self-centered mankind naively divided plants into the useful and the useless. In the same way it divided animals into those which were either domestic on the one hand or "game" on the other, and the "vermin" which ought to be destroyed. That was the day when extermination of whole species was taken as a matter of course and random introductions which usually proved to be either complete failures or all too successful were everywhere being made. Soon, however, it became evident enough that to rid the world of vermin and to stock it with nothing but useful organisms was at least not a simple task—if you assume that "useful" means simply "immediately useful to man."

Yet even to this day the *ideal* remains the same for most people. They may know, or at least they may have been told, that what looks like the useless is often remotely but demonstrably essential. Out in [the] desert country they may see the land being rendered useless by overuse. They may even have heard how, when the mountain lion is killed off, the deer multiply; how, when the deer multiply, the new growth of trees and shrubs is eaten away; and how, when the hills are denuded, a farm or a section of grazing land many miles away is washed into gulleys and made incapable of supporting either man or any other of the large animals. They may even have heard how the wonderful new insecticides proved so effective that fish and birds died of starvation; how on at least one Pacific island insects had to be reintroduced to pollinate the crops; how when you kill off almost completely a destructive pest, you run the risk of starving out everything which preys upon it and thus run the risk that the pest itself will stage an overwhelming comeback because its natural enemies are no more. Yet, knowing all this and much more, their dream is still the dream that an earth for man's use only can be created if only we learn more and scheme more effectively. They still hope that nature's scheme of checks and balances which provides for a varied population, which stubbornly refuses to scheme only from man's point of view and cherishes the weeds and "vermin" as persistently as she cherishes him, can be replaced by a scheme of his own devising. Ultimately they hope they can beat the game. But the more the ecologist learns, the less likely it seems that man can in the long run do anything of the sort. . . .

What is commonly called "conservation" will not work in the long run because it is not really conservation at all but rather, disguised by its elaborate scheming, only a more knowledgeable variation of the old idea of a world for man's use only. That idea is unrealizable. But how can man be persuaded to cherish any other ideal unless he can learn to take some interest and some delight in the beauty and variety of the world for its own sake, unless he can see a "value" in a flower blooming or an animal at play, unless he can see some "use" in things not useful?

In our society we pride ourselves upon having reached a point where we condemn an individual whose whole aim in life is to acquire material wealth for himself. But his vulgarity is only one step removed from that of a society which takes no thought for anything except increasing the material wealth of the community itself. In his usual extravagant way Thoreau once said: "This curious world which we inhabit is more wonderful than it is convenient; more beautiful than it is useful; it is more to be admired than it is to be used." Perhaps that "more" is beyond what most people could or perhaps ought to be convinced of. But without some realization that "this curious world" is at least beautiful as well as useful, "conservation" is doomed. We must live for something besides making a living. If we do not permit the earth to produce beauty and joy, it will in the end not produce food either.

Here practical considerations and those which are commonly called "moral," "aesthetic," and even "sentimental" join hands. Yet even the enlightened Department of Agriculture is so far from being fully enlightened that it encourages the farmer to forget that his land can ever produce anything except crops and is fanatical to the point of advising him how to build fences so that a field may be plowed to the last inch without leaving even that narrow margin in which one of the wild flowers—many of which agriculture has nearly rendered extinct—may continue to remind him that the world is beautiful as well as useful. And that brings us around to another of Aldo Leopold's seminal ideas:

> Conservation still proceeds at a snail's pace; . . . the usual answer . . . is "more conservation." . . . But is it certain that only the *volume* of education needs stepping up? Is something lacking in *content* as well? . . . It is inconceivable to me that an ethical relation to land can exist without love, respect and admiration for land, and a high regard for its value. By value, I of course mean something far broader than mere economic value; I mean value in the philosophical sense.

. . . A war more or less concealed under the guise of a "conflict of interests" rages between the "practical" conservationist and the defenders of national parks and other public lands; between cattlemen and lumberers on the one hand, and "sentimentalists" on the other. The pressure to allow the hunter, the rancher, or the woodcutter to invade the public domain is constant and the plea is always that we should "use" what is assumed to be useless unless it is adding to material welfare. But unless somebody teaches love, there can be no ultimate protection to what is lusted after. Without some "love of nature" for itself there is no possibility of solving "the problem of conservation."

Any fully matured science of ecology will have to grapple with the fact that from the ecological point of view, man is one of those animals which is in danger from its too successful participation in the struggle for existence. He has upset the balance of nature to a point where he has exterminated hundreds of other animals and exhausted soils. Part of this he calls a demonstration of his intelligence and of the success which results from his use of it. But because of that intelligence he has learned how to exploit resources very thoroughly and he is even beginning to learn how to redress the balance in certain minor ways. But he cannot keep indefinitely just one step ahead of overcrowding and starvation. From the standpoint of nature as a whole, he is both a threat to every other living thing and, therefore, a threat to himself also. If he were not so extravagantly successful it would be better for nearly everything except man and, possibly therefore, better, in the longest run, for him also. He has become the tyrant of the earth, the waster of its resources, the creator of the most prodigious imbalance in the natural order which has ever existed.

From a purely homocentric point of view this may seem entirely proper. To most people it undoubtedly does. Is it not our proudest boast that we have learned how to "control nature"? Does not our dream of the future include a final emancipation from any dependence upon a natural balance and the substitution for it of some balance established by ourselves and in our exclusive interest? Is not that, in fact, what most people have in mind when they think of the final triumph of humanity?

But what every "practical" ecologist is trying to do is maintain the balance of nature without facing the fact that man himself is part of it, that you cannot hope to keep the balance unless you admit that to some extent the immediate interest of the human species may sometimes have to be disregarded. No other single fact is so important as man himself in creating the often disastrous imbalances which continually develop. It is not possible to reestablish them for long without undertaking to control the organism which has most obviously entered upon a runaway phase. Must we not recognize the fact that any real "management of resources" is impossible unless we are willing to sacrifice to some extent the immediate interests not only of certain individual men but also those of the human species itself? Most of us have reached the point where we recognize that the immediate interests of the lumberman or the rancher must sometimes be sacrificed to "the general good." Ultimately we may have to recognize that there is also a conflict between what is called the general good and a good still more general—the good, that is to say, of the whole biological community. . . .

The now popular saying, "No man is an island," means more than it is commonly taken to mean. Not only men but all living things stand or fall together. Or rather man is of all such creatures one of those least able to stand alone. If we think only in terms of our own welfare we are likely to find that we are losing it.

But how can man learn to accept such a situation, to believe that it is right and proper when the whole tendency of his thought and his interest carries him in a contrary direction? How can he learn to value and delight in a natural order larger than his own order? How can he come to accept, not sullenly but gladly, the necessity of sharing the earth?

As long ago as the seventeenth century, as long ago, that is, as the very time when the ambition to "control nature" in any large ambitious way was first coming to be formulated and embraced, a sort of answer to these questions was being given in theological terms. John Ray, one of the first great English biologists, formulated them in a book which was read for a hundred years, and what Ray had to say cuts two ways because it was directed against the egotism of man as expressed both by the old-fashioned theologians who thought that everything had been *made* for man's use and by the Baconians who assumed that he could at least *turn it* to that use.

"It is," Ray wrote, "a general received opinion, that all this visible world was created for Man; that Man is the End of Creation; as if there were no other end of any creature, but some way or other to be serviceable to man. . . . But though this be vulgarly received, yet wise men now-a-days think otherwise. Dr. Moore affirms, that creatures are made to enjoy themselves as well as to serve us." The greatest profit which we can get from the observation and study of other living things is, Ray went on to say, often not that we learn how to use them but that we may contemplate through them the wonders and the beauties of God's creation. What Ray was saying is precisely that Thoreay was restating in secularized form when he insisted that "this curious world . . . is more to be admired and enjoyed than it is to be used."

Since our age is not inclined to be interested in theological arguments, it is not likely to find Ray's exposition a sufficient reason for accepting gladly the continued existence on this earth of "useless" plants and animals occupying space which man might turn to his own immediate profit. Our generation is more likely to make at least certain concessions in that direction as the result of absorbing what the ecologist has to say about the impossibility of maintaining a workable balance without a much more generous view of what is "useful" and what is not. But it is not certain that on that basis man will ever make quite enough concessions and it *is* entirely certain that he will not make them happily, will not find life pleasanter just because he makes them, unless he can learn to love and to delight in the variety of nature.

Perhaps, if we cannot send him as far back as the seventeenth century to be taught, we can at least send him back to the eighteenth. Pope, speaking half for metaphysics and half for science, could write:

> Has God, thou fool! work'd solely for thy good,
> Thy joy, thy pastime, thy attire, thy food?
>   .   .   .   .   .   .
>
> Know, Nature's children all divide her care;
> The fur that warms a monarch, warm'd a bear.

This is precisely what most men even two centuries later do not really understand.

René Dubos

Is Survival Enough?

Adaptability is an asset for biological survival, but paradoxically, the greatest threat to the quality of human life is that the human species is so immensely adaptable that it can survive even under the most objectionable conditions.

There is much evidence that tolerance of undesirable conditions is achieved at the cost of physical and mental disabilities later in life. To a large extent, the so-called diseases of civilization are the delayed consequences of biological and mental stresses to which the organism has made adaptive responses that appear effective at the time they occur, but are inadequate in the long run.

The words soil, air, water, freedom are loaded with emotional content because they are associated with biological and mental needs that are woven in the fabric of man's nature. These needs are as vital today as they were in the distant past. Scientists and economists may learn a great deal about the intricacies of physicochemical phenomena, biological processes, and cost accounting. But scientific knowledge of environmental management will contribute little to health and happiness if it continues to neglect the human values symbolized by phrases such as the good earth, a brilliant sky, sparkling waters, a place of one's own. A true science of human life should concern itself with the maintenance and enlargement of the values that the eighteenth century associated with the word "civilization." . . .

Throughout the eighteenth century the word "civilization" had a far more restricted meaning than we give it now. It referred to gentle ways of life, humane laws, limitations on war, a high level of purpose and conduct, in brief, all the qualities considered to be the highest expressions of mankind. . . .

. . . The essential genetic aspects of [man's] body and brain were shaped by the environmental forces that prevailed on earth during his evolutionary past. Furthermore, as far as can be judged, man's genetic makeup has not changed significantly since the Old Stone Age. In the words of the English anthropologist Jacquetta Hawkes, "The psyche which lives in every human being as the generations rise and fall has not been totally transformed. It makes an unbroken chain between present and past. The bodily experiences opened to the men and women of thousands of years ago were identical with those of today; the mental and emotional ones were not altogether different."

The modern environment naturally exposes man to conditions very different from those under which he evolved. To a certain extent genetic readaptation to new environmental forces can take place because the huge range of potentialities that have accumulated in the human gene pool during the evolutionary past can be

From *Reason Awake: Science for Man* by René Dubos (New York: Columbia University Press, 1970), pp. 167-168, 159, 185-192. Reprinted by permission.

redistributed and selected to produce a rapid genetic drift whenever the selection pressure is strong enough. But, wide as man's variability may be, it is limited by the instructions encoded in his genetic equipment. Scientific civilization must therefore concern itself with the genetic limits of man's tolerance, because these determine the range within which social and technological changes are compatible with his life.

Immunity and allergy (in the usual sense of the word) are the two best-studied types of lasting changes that the environment can elicit in man. But they are not the only ones, nor even the most important. . . . Most aspects of the body and the mind can be altered almost irreversibly by the organism's responses to almost any stimulus. For this reason the quality of the environment cannot be judged only from its present effects; the delayed and indirect effects may be more important in the long run.

It has been shown, for example, that a single injection into newborn mice of particulate materials separated from urban air greatly increases the frequency of various types of tumors during the adult life of these animals. If this observation can be extrapolated and applied to human beings, the worst consequences of pollution are yet to be recognized, since it is only during the past two decades that babies born and raised in urban areas have been exposed to high levels of pollutants.

If present trends continue most people in the world will soon live in large urban agglomerations. Massive urbanization would have disastrous biological consequences if it were not for the fact that the majority of urban dwellers develop some form of tolerance to environmental pollutants, intense sensory stimuli, and high population density, just as they develop herd immunity to ubiquitous microbial pathogens. However, such acquired tolerance may not be an unmixed blessing, because it is often the expression of undesirable functional changes. For example, continuous exposure to low levels of air pollutants stimulates mucous secretion in the walls of the tracheobronchial tree, thus affording some protection to the pulmonary epithelium. But eventually the cumulative effects of irritation result in chronic bronchitis and other forms of irreversible pulmonary damage.

Recent physiological and behavioral studies have revealed that people born and raised in an environment where food intake is quantitatively or qualitatively inadequate achieve a certain form of physiologic and behavioral adaptation to low-food intake. They tend to restrict their physical and mental activity and thereby reduce their nutritional needs; in other words, they become adjusted to undernutrition by living less intensely. Furthermore, they retain throughout their lives the physiological and mental imprinting caused by early nutritional deprivation. Physical apathy and indolence have long been assumed to have a racial or climatic origin. In reality, these behavioral traits often constitute a form of physiologic adjustment to malnutrition, especially when nutritional scarcity has been experienced very early in life.

Undernutrition is now rare in affluent countries, but malnutrition can take many other forms, including perhaps excessive artificial feeding of the infant. Little is known of the biological and psychological effects that result from a nutritional regimen which differs qualitatively from that of the mother's milk and exceeds it quantitatively, but there is evidence that infants fed an extremely rich and abundant diet tend to become large eaters as adults. Such acquired dietary habits are probably objectionable from the physiological point of view; it would be surprising if they did not have behavioral manifestations.

Crowding and constant exposure to social stimuli are inevitable accompaniments of urbanization and are usually regarded as deleterious. Human beings, however, can become adapted to crowding, especially if they have been exposed to it during the early phases of their development—just as they can become tolerant to most other types of stressful situations. Adaptation to crowding has been observed in laboratory animals and in human populations.

Experiments in various animal species have revealed that crowding commonly results in disturbances in endocrine function and behavior. But the intensity of the effects is profoundly influenced by the conditions under which high population density is achieved. When adult animals of a given species are brought together in a confined environment, they exhibit aggressive behavior and a large percentage of them may die. In contrast, if a few animals are placed in a given enclosure and allowed to multiply in it, the population to which they give rise can reach very high density without evidence of destructive aggressiveness. While growing together the animals achieve a social organization that minimizes violent conflict. Beyond a certain level of population density more and more animals exhibit abnormal behavior, but in general these deviants are not sick organically. They act as if they were unaware of the presence of their cage mates; their behavior is asocial rather than antisocial.

Men are not rats, yet the most unpleasant thing about overcrowded rats is that they behave so much like human beings in some crowded communities. Man has developed a variety of social mechanisms that enable him to live at high-population densities; for example, Hong Kong and Holland show us that such densities are compatible with physical health and low crime rates. However, there are other human communities in which extreme crowding leads to a kind of asocial behavior very similar to the social unawareness manifested in overcrowded animal populations.

In most cases the deleterious effects of crowding result not so much from high population density as from the social disturbances associated with *sudden* increases in density. The appalling amount of physical and mental disease during the first phase of the Industrial Revolution was caused in large part by poor sanitation and malnutrition, but certainly another important factor was that immense numbers of people from rural areas migrated within a few decades to the new industrial cities. They had to live and function in the crowded slums and shops of the teeming industrial cities before they could make physiological and emotional adjustments. Yet it took but a few decades to convert these rural populations into urban ones, which now find satisfaction in the crowds that precipitated biological and mental diseases a century ago.

Because of my professional specialization and also probably because our society is disease-conscious, the pathological aspects of response to the environment have been emphasized; but there are other psychological aspects which are at least as interesting and socially important.

In the modern industrial city human beings hardly ever have the chance to see the Milky Way or a night radiant with stars or even a truly blue sky. They never experience the subtle fragrances peculiar to each season, the exhilaration of early spring and the poetic melancholy of autumn. The loss of these experiences may be more than an esthetic deprivation; certain emotional needs were woven in man's fabric during his evolutionary past, and their satisfaction may well be required for complete biological and mental sanity.

Other kinds of undesirable changes are likely to occur as a result of extreme urbanization. The complexity of social structures makes some form of regimentation unavoidable; freedom and privacy may come to constitute antisocial luxuries, and even to involve hardships. As a consequence the human beings most likely to prosper in congested urban environments will be those willing to accept a regimented life in a teeming world from which all wilderness and fantasy will have disappeared. The domesticated farm animals and the laboratory rodents on controlled nutritional regimens in controlled environments will then become true models for the study of man.

Admittedly, it is possible to rear and train children for oversocialized conditions—to such an extent that they do not feel safe and happy outside a crowd of their own kind. But this does not invalidate the view that there is potential danger in increased urban crowding. Children and even adults can be trained to accept as desirable almost any form of perversion—physiological, behavioral, or intellectual.

In the final analysis, the human environment is what man experiences, and it is the quality of this experience that shapes individuality and gives its value to life. For this reason one feels sorrow and indignation at seeing the children in American cities being continuously exposed to noise, ugliness, and garbage in the street—and thereby conditioned to accept public squalor as the normal state of affairs.

Winston Churchill expressed in a memorable phrase that the environment has a deep and lasting influence on human beings: "We shape our buildings and afterwards, our buildings shape us." In even more telling and moving words, James Baldwin has repeatedly affirmed his conviction that [Black Americans are shaped by their life experiences, especially the early ones]:

> We cannot escape our origins, however hard we try, those origins which contain the key—could we but find it—to all that we later become.
> It means something to live where one sees space and sky or to live where one sees nothing but rubble or nothing but high buildings.
> We take our shape . . . within and against that cage of reality bequeathed us at our birth.[1]

1. James Baldwin, *Notes of a Native Son* (New York: Dial Press, 1963).

The Spaceship Earth is the cage within and against which man has developed in his evolutionary past and continues to develop his biological and mental characteristics. As the terrestrial environment deteriorates so does humanness and the quality of human life.

Admittedly, human beings are so adaptable that they can survive, function, and multiply despite malnutrition, environmental pollution, excessive sensory stimuli, ugliness, and boredom, high population density and its attendant regimentation. But while biological adaptability is an asset for the survival of *Homo sapiens* considered as a biological species, it can be fatal to the attributes that make human life different from animal life. From the human point of view environmental quality and the success of adaptation must be judged in terms of values peculiar to man.